"This book is balanced and captivating. It guides the reader through a clear, comprehensive, and grounded review of the knowledge and practices in the area of family systems. A great resource for family researchers, educators, and clinicians seeking to advance their work."
— **Sesen Negash, PhD, LMFT,** *associate professor and director, Marriage and Family Therapy Program, San Diego State University*

"In *The Science of Family Systems Theory*, Dr. Priest provides a cohesive guide to understanding and applying general systems theory with increased clarity and purpose. From describing the minute details of cells and DNA within the body to explaining systemic oppression in broader sociocultural systems, the author provides the reader with an opportunity to see how comprehensive general systems theory can be in explaining so many processes in the universe. The book also provides examples of how to make clear connections between scientific observations and family systems theory."
— **Daniel Hubler, PhD, CFLE,** *associate professor, Child and Family Studies, Weber State University*

The Science of Family Systems Theory

This accessible text examines how the science of autonomy and adaptation informs all family therapy approaches and discusses how clinicians can use this science to improve their practice.

Uniquely focusing on how to integrate science and theory into clinical practice, the book provides an overview of science from multiple domains and ties it to family systems theory through the key framework of autonomy and adaptation. Drawing on research from genetics, physiology, emotion regulation, attachment, and triangulation, chapters demonstrate how a comprehensive science-informed theory of family systems can be applied to a range of problematic family patterns. The text also explores self-of-the-therapist work and considers how autonomy and attachment are connected to systems of power, privilege, and oppression.

Supported throughout by practical case examples, as well as questions for consideration, chapter summaries, and resource lists to further engage the reader, *The Science of Family Systems Theory* is an essential textbook for marriage and family therapy students as well as mental health professionals working with families.

Jacob B. Priest is an associate professor in the couple and family therapy program at the University of Iowa. He received a PhD from Florida State University and has a private practice at the Counseling Center of Iowa City.

The Science of Family Systems Theory

Jacob B. Priest

Routledge
Taylor & Francis Group
NEW YORK AND LONDON

First published 2021
by Routledge
52 Vanderbilt Avenue, New York, NY 10017

and by Routledge
2 Park Square, Milton Park, Abingdon, Oxon, OX14 4RN

Routledge is an imprint of the Taylor & Francis Group, an informa business

© 2021 Jacob B. Priest

The right of Jacob B. Priest to be identified as author of this work has been asserted by him in accordance with sections 77 and 78 of the Copyright, Designs and Patents Act 1988.

All rights reserved. No part of this book may be reprinted or reproduced or utilised in any form or by any electronic, mechanical, or other means, now known or hereafter invented, including photocopying and recording, or in any information storage or retrieval system, without permission in writing from the publishers.

Trademark notice: Product or corporate names may be trademarks or registered trademarks, and are used only for identification and explanation without intent to infringe.

Library of Congress Cataloging-in-Publication Data
Names: Priest, Jacob Bird, author.
Title: The science of family systems theory / Jacob B. Priest.
Description: New York, NY : Routledge, 2021. | Includes bibliographical references and index. |
Summary: "This accessible text examines how the science of autonomy and adaptation inform all family therapy approaches and discusses how clinicians can use this science to improve their practice. Supported throughout by practical case examples, as well as questions for consideration, chapter summaries, and resource lists to further engage the reader, The Science of Family Systems is an essential textbook for marriage and family therapy students as well as mental health professionals working with families"— Provided by publisher.
Identifiers: LCCN 2020043550 (print) | LCCN 2020043551 (ebook) | ISBN 9780367427160 (hardback) | ISBN 9780367427184 (paperback) | ISBN 9780367854591 (ebook)
Subjects: LCSH: Systemic therapy (Family therapy) | Family psychotherapy.
Classification: LCC RC488.5 .P75 2021 (print) | LCC RC488.5 (ebook) | DDC 616.89/156—dc23
LC record available at https://lccn.loc.gov/2020043550
LC ebook record available at https://lccn.loc.gov/2020043551

ISBN: 978-0-367-42716-0 (hbk)
ISBN: 978-0-367-42718-4 (pbk)
ISBN: 978-0-367-85459-1 (ebk)

Typeset in Sabon
by Apex CoVantage, LLC

To Chelsea and Keenan

Contents

Acknowledgments	xi
1 An Introduction to Family Systems Theory	1

PART 1
The Evidence of Autonomy and Adaptation — 13

2 The Genetic and Individual Systems	15
3 The Attachment, Triangulation, and Family Systems	31
4 The Sociocultural System	48

PART 2
Linking the Evidence to Theory — 63

5 The Family as an Autonomous System	65
6 The Family as an Adaptable System	75
7 Family Systems Theory Revisited	83

PART 3
Linking Theory to Practice — 99

8 The Postmodern Critique and Family Systems Theory	101
9 Attachment Theory and Family Systems Theory	108

10 Trauma in Family Systems Theory	117
11 Family Systems Theory and Family Therapy Models	131
12 Conclusions and Recommendations	140
Appendix A: Read Better	146
Appendix B: Engage Differently	158
Bibliography	160
Index	173

Acknowledgments

This book would not have been possible without the help and support of many. Lorna Hecker, thank you for making the introductions and helping me think this was possible. Thank you to my Editors at Routledge – Clare Ashworth, for getting it off the ground and Heather Evans for seeing it through the finish line. Volker Thomas, thank you for your careful reading and thoughtful suggestions – the book is much better because of it. Sarah Woods and Patricia Roberson, thank you for being sounding boards and idea generators. Thank you Armeda Wojciak and Kayla Reed-Fitzke. I couldn't ask for better colleagues or friends. And thank you to the teachers, professors, mentors, and clients who have inspired and challenged me.

My parents, Scott and Sally, and my siblings, Shanna, Brody, Eli, Sarryn, and Saydie have been my champions since I entered the world of family therapy. None of this would have been possible without their support. To the world's best cat, Albert – thank you for keeping me company in the office during long writing days. Finally, I am fortunate to be married to someone who writes far better than I can. Chelsea, thank you for being my first and best editor and for the incredible support you provided throughout this process. I love you and I like you.

Chapter 1

An Introduction to Family Systems Theory

When people ask me about my job, I lie – a little bit. When someone asks me what I do, I say, "I'm a family therapist."

More often than not, they then ask, "So, like a psychologist?"

This is when I lie. I say, "Yes, like a psychologist."

It's not a total lie. Like many psychologists or counselors, I do psychotherapy. People come to me when issues or problems come up. They come into my office, we talk about these issues, and we work together to tackle their problems. But my training and way of thinking about their problems are different. As a family therapist, my practice is rooted in family systems theory. This theory is what sets me apart from other psychologists and counselors. It's what makes family therapists family therapists.

The State of Family Systems Theory

In *Family Evaluation* (1988), Michael Kerr and Murray Bowen argued that "human behavior is significantly regulated by the same natural processes that regulate the behavior of all other living things" (p. 3). They sought to place the human family in the context of biological science. Throughout their book, the pair drew upon the best available research to demonstrate how evolution and other processes had shaped the family system and could explain the development of problems in families. This was their basis for their family systems theory.

In laying out their theory, they acknowledged that the science of factors that regulate human behavior and the family systems was limited. They suggested that with new knowledge, their ideas about the family system would require adapting or amending. They saw their work as a first step in understanding the family as a natural system, but they noted that researchers had "barely scratched the surface" in uncovering what shapes human behavior and family interactions.

More than 30 years later, the knowledge we have regarding family systems has grown substantially. We now understand more about biological processes such as evolution and genetics and their effect on family systems. We know more about the human brain and body and the role that emotion and attachment play in families. Researchers have uncovered factors associated with loving, committed, healthy relationships, and we know more about how broader sociopolitical forces affect families. If in Kerr and Bowen's era, the science of family systems had "barely scratched the surface," today, we have broken through the surface and begun to dig into the core.

But with all this new knowledge, family systems theory has gotten stuck. Karen Wampler and her colleagues (2019) noted that the field of family therapy is still largely reliant on the family systems proposals of people like Murry Bowen, Salvador Minuchin, and Virginia Satir – most are more than 30 years old. They pointed out that, to move the field forward, the hypotheses that accompany family systems theory need to be scrutinized by research. By scrutinizing these hypotheses, we may be able to create greater innovation in systemic family therapy practice.

Theory and research are supposed to have a reciprocal relationship. Theory drives research hypotheses. Research findings provide evidence for or opposition to the hypotheses. Based on the evidence, the theory is supported, adjusted, or discarded. But this hasn't happened with family systems theory. Though the understanding of the science of family systems has grown exponentially, this evidence we have gained hasn't been applied to the hypotheses of family systems theory. In other words, family systems theory hasn't been assessed by the new evidence.

Evidence-Based Practice and Practice-Based Evidence

One reason that family systems theory hasn't been updated is that researchers, with good reason, have been focusing on family therapy outcomes. Researchers have been seeking to answer the question, "Does family therapy work?" This research, often referred to as evidence-based practice, has provided good evidence that it does. When people work with a family therapist, they tend to get better (Shadish & Baldwin, 2003). We have evidence that family therapy works for childhood problems such as behavioral issues, emotional problems, eating disorders, and many others (Carr, 2014a). We also have evidence that family therapy works for adult problems, including marital distress, sexual dysfunction, intimate partner violence, depression, anxiety, and adjusting to chronic illnesses (Carr, 2014b). Evidence gathered through randomized control trials has found that specific models including functional family therapy (Sexton, 2017) or solution-focused therapy (Gingerich, Kim, Stams, & MacDonald, 2012) help clients reach their goals.

Another area of research, practice-based evidence, is concerned with the question: *What makes a good family therapist?* The research addressing this question has led to the development of many tools to help therapists get better. Lee Johnson and his colleagues have developed the Marriage and Family Therapy Practice Network (Johnson, Miller, Bradford, & Anderson, 2017). This network provides therapists with assessments that get client feedback and track client growth over time with the goal of improving outcomes. Evidence suggests that when therapists solicit feedback and track client progress, outcomes improve (e.g., Anker, Duncan, & Sparks, 2009; Shimokawa, Lambert, & Smart, 2010). Researchers and practitioners are studying and adapting the research to refine the practice of family therapy; helping to identify what individual therapists bring into the room that help clients get better.

These two research areas have done a great deal to advance the practice of family therapy. Today, therapists have clear ways to improve their practice, and most importantly, they can provide care to their clients grounded in evidence. Though there needs to be continued improvement in evidence-based practice and practice-based evidence (e.g., Dattilio, Piercy, & Davis, 2014; Wittenborn, Blow, Holtrop, & Parra-Cardona, 2019), the evidence we have about our models and our work continues to advance. However, this evidence is skill- and model-based – it's not focused on supporting the proposals of a theory.

Though these avenues of evidence have added much to the field of family therapy, there needs to be a renewed focus on family systems theory. If we don't continue to revise family systems theory, based on new evidence, we risk the assumptions of our approaches becoming invalid. If we aren't keeping up on the science, we risk being left behind or not being viewed as part of the mainstream of therapeutic practice. Though we know family therapy works, by validating family systems theory based on current scientific knowledge, we can do things that work better. We may develop evidence-based treatments that work better than the ones we currently have, and we can spur innovation and creativity both in individual therapists and throughout the field.

What Is Family Systems Theory?

Family systems theory is surprisingly difficult to define. If you ask ten family therapists to define it, you won't get a consistent answer. When I ask my students or my colleagues to define it, I get a variety of responses. Some have said things like, "It's the idea that family members' actions and emotions are connected," or similarly, the idea that "the whole is greater than the sum of its parts." Others start talking about the model they use or their own "theory of change."

Family therapy researchers also don't have a clear definition of family systems theory. In a review of 275 family therapy research studies, 28 different theories of models were identified as used by family therapy researchers (Chen, Hughes, & Austin, 2017). Some used "systems theory," but poorly defined it; others used models or "mid-level theories" that are connected to family systems theory but failed to tie the two together. The authors of this review article noted that for family therapy researchers, "Simply stating that a study is guided by a systemic perspective or family systems theory overlooks an opportunity to enlighten the reader on the nuances of theory, as well as extend the theory itself" (Chen et al., 2017, p. 522). In other words, because family systems theory is often defined poorly or in different ways, it's hard to have a clear definition of what family systems theory is.

Defining Family Systems Theory

So, let's define it. To build a working definition of family systems theory, let's break it apart and take a look at each part individually – starting with "theory."

A theory is a set of testable hypotheses that explains facts about the real world. A theory is not a "best guess," a perspective, or a speculation. It is a documented set of proposals that can be proven false. For example, atomic theory is a set of hypotheses that predicts how atoms interact, form compounds, and behave. Initially, atomic theory was speculative, but as researchers tested the predictions of this theory the evidence for these principles became apparent. Though we couldn't see atoms until 1981, most scientists supported atomic theory long before that due to the vast amount of evidence supporting the hypotheses (Coyne, 2010).

Atomic theory also underscores the close connection between theory and research. The hypotheses of a theory are tested empirically – using multiple research methods. If the results of the empirical tests show evidence for a hypothesis, that hypothesis becomes supported. If empirical tests of a hypothesis can be replicated over and over again, we then refer to this hypothesis as scientific fact. But, if we test a hypothesis, and there isn't evidence supporting it, we must then change or discard the hypothesis and its accompanying theory. In the case of atomic theory, the way it was originally proposed is different than how we understand it now. As researchers tested the hypotheses of atomic theory, they found evidence for major parts of the theory, but others were not supported. As such, atomic theory was adjusted on the basis of the new evidence.

A theory is also different from a model. Atomic theory predicts and explains the function of atoms, yet scientists and researchers use multiple models to test, examine, and manipulate atomic compounds. In the same way, family systems theory is different from family therapy models. Many family therapy models are based on family systems theory, but they use different techniques, approaches, and interventions to manipulate the family system.

With this definition of theory, let's now define "system." Ludwig von Bertalanffy is often considered as one of the originators of systems theory. In his book, *General Systems Theory*, he defined systems and delineated the hypotheses of systems theory. He defined a system as "a set of elements standing in inter-relations" (p. 55). For elements to be inter-related, he argued, the interactions of elements within a system must be different from interactions of elements outside of the system. He then described the hypotheses of systems theory based on this definition. Since von Bertalanffy proposed his theory, his hypotheses have been tested. While many of his hypotheses have been supported, others have been revised by the results of research. Systems theory looks different today than it did when von Bertalanffy first proposed it.

What, then, is family systems theory? Let's start with defining our system of interest, the "family" system. If we draw on von Bertalanffy's definition of a system, the family system is a set of humans who stand in interrelations to one another. When we talk about families, this "interrelation" typically occurs through blood, mating, or adoption – though many family systems include people who don't fit that criterion. The basic definition of family systems theory would then be a *theory that proposes testable predictions about interrelated people*. And, to extend it a bit more, it is *a theory that predicts and explains how people within a family system interact, and how interactions inside the family system are different from those outside of it*.

Which Family Systems Theory?

With this definition of family systems theory, we need to examine the hypotheses of this theory. When you try to find testable predictions regarding family systems, it can be overwhelming. Remember, family therapy researchers have used as many as 28 different theories to explain family systems, each having its own hypotheses about the family system. In 2016, Alan Carr listed 20 proposals of family systems theory. This included things like: 1. The family is a social system that supports the survival and welfare of its members; 2. The family is a system with boundaries and is organized into subsystems; 3. The boundary around the family sets it apart from the wider social and cultural systems; 4. Patterns of family interaction are rule governed and recursive; 5. The overall patterning of rule-governed family relationships may be described in terms of family roles, routines, and rituals; 6. Within the family there are processes that both prevent and promote change; and 7. Patterns in the family system are isomorphic – patterns present in one part of the system are present in other parts of the system.

Though this is an exhaustive list, it still ignores important hypotheses like those put forward by Michael Kerr and Murry Bowen. They proposed that the family system was governed by three other systems: 1. The emotional system – a naturally occurring system that allows all organisms to receive, integrate, and respond to information within itself and from the environment; 2. The feeling system – the system in which humans experience guilt, shame, sympathy, ecstasy, rejection, or sadness; and 3. The intellectual system – which allows humans to have the capacity to know and understand. Kerr and Bowen suggest that these systems are governed by the life forces of individuality and togetherness, which lead to patterned behavior and emotional reactivity. The ability to manage individuality and togetherness in a family system is called differentiation of self. Greater differentiation of self results in better relationships and fewer clinical problems.

But why is it so hard to get a clear answer about what family systems theory is? Why are there 28 or more theories used when doing family systems research? And why do we need more than 20 hypotheses to describe family systems theory?

One reason for these multiple, overlapping, hypotheses is that family systems theory and its proposals have drawn on different epistemologies. In addition to drawing on von Bertalanffy's systems ideas and other biological concepts, family systems theory also draws on ideas from Cybernetics – the study of control and communication in humans, other animals, and machines (Wiener, 1949). However, as Robert Vallee (2003) pointed out, cybernetics and systems, though different, also share many similarities. This is evident in the overlap we see in the hypotheses of family systems theory. Each of these proposals is describing the processes that create the family system. They talk about boundary making, rules, the differentiation of subsystems within the family, and how the family system reacts and responds to stress. If we were to examine other hypotheses used in family systems research, we would see a similar pattern. Though they might use different words or ideas to describe these processes, they are getting at most of the same ideas.

I think good theory and good science happen when hypotheses are clear, succinct, and testable. Good theories are logically consistent and can explain and predict what they are intended to (White, Klein, & Martin, 2015). In other words, I think family systems theory needs to be reevaluated. We need clear hypotheses that can bring together the disparate research and epistemologies that inform family systems theory as well as refocus the disparate models that family therapists practice (Fife, 2020). We need a consensus about what family systems theory is, so we can refine and improve the theory and thereby potentially refine and improve our practice.

To do this, we need to return to where we began – general systems theory. Though family systems theory has drawn from cybernetics and other areas of science, I would argue that general systems theory provides the strongest foundation for family systems theory. General systems theory has been used to describe multiple biological systems and has been used to unify scientific research across many disciplines. In addition, many of the concepts of cybernetics grew out of or can be folded into a general systems approach (Vallee, 2003). By tying family systems theory into the research and science of general systems theory, we can connect it to the broader biological sciences.

Just like atomic theory and many other theories before it, general systems theory has evolved. The concepts and ideas that von Bertalanffy originally proposed have been rigorously studied and updated. Today, systems researchers and theorists are focused on hypotheses related to two concepts – autonomy and adaptation. These concepts are built on von Bertalanffy's work; however, based on new evidence that has come about since von Bertalanffy's proposals, some of his original hypotheses have been changed.

Autonomy and Adaptation

In the broadest sense, autonomy is how a system distinguishes itself from its environment while adaptation is how a system responds to its environment. In his book, *On the Origin of Autonomy*, Bernd Rosslenbroich (2014) describes autonomy and adaptation in systems. He proposes that living systems are autonomous when they:

> (1) Generate, maintain, and regulate an inner network of interdependent, energy-consuming processes, which in turn generate and maintain the system; (2) Establish a boundary and actively regulate their interactions and exchange with the environment; (3) Specify their own rules of behavior and react to stimuli in a self-determined way, according to their internal disposition and condition; (4) Establish an interdependence between the system and its part within the organism, which includes a differentiation of subsystems; (5) Establish time autonomy; and (6) Maintain . . . stability (robustness) in the face of diverse perturbations arising from the environmental changes, internal variability, and genetic variations.

Further he discusses adaptation and its relationship to autonomy, showing how adaptation is built into his ideas of autonomy.

> Adaptedness is a relational property of an organism or rather a property of the organism-environment system. . . . [A]utonomy and

> adaption become a central pair of this system. Both are dependent on each other: On the one hand, there is the organism, and on the other hand is the environment. The organisms – even in its simplest form – always establishes its life function together with the generation of a boundary and thus produces its "being different" from the surrounding environment. To maintain this state, the organism not only needs to regulatory and stabilizing functions on the one hand but needs to react appropriately to cope successfully with the environmental influences ... autonomy needs adaptations.
>
> (pp. 230–231)

Rosslenbroich is proposing that systems require both autonomy and adaptation and that the two depend on each other. Systems need the properties of autonomy, but these properties stand in relation to and a property of the adaptations necessary to survive in an environment. The presence of autonomy only exists by it being distinguished from its environment; yet the very process of distinguishing itself is an adaptation.

Similar arguments have been made by other scholars. In 2018, Anne Sophie Meincke's review of relevant research supported the ideas of Rosslenbroich. She suggested:

> Living systems are nested hierarches of processes which are more or less stable depending on the time scale at which they are described, and depending on which other processes they are camparted with... Any stability to be observed in living systems is the result of continuous process and change.
>
> (p. 13)

And in 2019, she argued further:

> Organisms, human and non-human, are dynamical systems that for their existence and persistence depend on an on-going interaction with the environment in which they are embedded.... We cannot understand what organisms are, and how they persist through time, if not acknowledging their genuine dynamicity, fluidity, and constitutive changeability.
>
> (p. 57)

She is arguing that autonomy and adaptation are the key organizing and operating processes of systems. Systemic autonomy comes from the stable process that occurs across time, and at the same time, the processes that create the system are constantly interacting with the environment and therefore must adapt.

Along those same lines, Alvaro Moreno and Matteo Mossio suggested, in their book *Biological Autonomy*, that:

> The framework we have proposed is centered on the idea of autonomy. Our main claim that the distinctive feature of biological systems, which distinguishes them from any other natural system, is their autonomy. Biological systems are autonomous, which means that, in the most general sense, that they contribute to the generation and maintenance of the conditions of their existence. . . . As a result of their agency, autonomous systems interact with each other, mutually affecting their respective organization and constituting higher-level collective autonomous organizations, without losing their autonomy. These higher levels of autonomy can in turn generate new networks of interactions, which can possibly lead to even higher levels of autonomy.
>
> (p. 197)

They assert that autonomy is the core feature of any living system. But that these systems interact and affect each other and that these interactions lead to adaptations that can create new systems.

Each of these systems thinkers has reviewed the evidence and concurs that living systems are best understood and described through autonomy and adaptation. Autonomy and adaptation can pull together ideas from evolution, biology, and physiology to predict and describe how systems function.

Family Systems Theory Hypotheses

If we return to the summary of proposals made by Alan Carr, we can see that they fit easily into the concepts of autonomy and adaptation. These hypotheses describe boundary making and the internal processes that sustain these boundaries – how family systems develop and maintain autonomy. It also offers proposals on rules and patterns and how boundaries are crossed in systems – how they adapt. Similarly, Bowen's hypotheses describe how family systems incorporate autonomy and adaptation – the concepts of individuality and togetherness are key players in family system autonomy. The emotional, feeling, and intellectual systems talk about ways in which the family system responds to the environment, and the process of differentiation describes the tension and reciprocity between autonomy and adaptation. In other words, autonomy and adaptation can be used to unify and clarify the many proposals of family systems theory and their underlying epistemologies.

With this in mind, we can simplify family systems theory to just two hypotheses. The first is that *the family is an autonomous system*. Family systems have rule-based, boundary-making processes that generate and maintain the family. These processes are distinct to the family system, occur across time, and remain relatively stable. The second is that *the family is an adaptable system*. The family system responds to stress from inside and outside of the system by making changes to its rule-based, boundary-making processes. The goal of these adaptations is to help the family maintain autonomy.

But are these two hypotheses valid? If they are, then evidence should be available to support these assertions. This evidence should be able to explain how these interactions create boundaries and responses, and why these boundaries and responses are unique to the family system. In other words, do scientific findings support the proposal that a family is an autonomous and adaptable system? What's more, if the family system is autonomous and adaptable, what are the important processes, boundaries, rules, and reactions that create autonomy while also allowing for adaptation?

If we understand these things, we can then better link family systems theory and its supporting evidence to the models of family therapy. We may then be able to develop better evidence-based practices. In addition, by providing evidence for family systems theory, we may be better able to link science and theory to our own practice, resulting in better outcomes for our clients.

The "Why" of This Book

Family systems theory is what sets family therapy apart from other psychotherapy approaches. Family systems theory is the foundation of the field, and it's the driver of family therapy models. For our field to remain strong, we need researchers to focus on developing and improving evidence-based practices as well as find ways to improve how we train therapists. But we also need a research and practice that is grounded in a scientifically validated theory. Without a strong, scientifically supported theory to ground our practice, we risk our models and practice becoming outdated. Theories remain strong only when the hypotheses of the theory are clear, testable, and supported by evidence.

The goal of this book is to outline the science that is linked to family systems theory. Specifically, we will explore the science relating to the hypotheses that the family is an autonomous and adaptable system. By examining the science of family systems, we can see if the evidence supports these hypotheses. Given the vast amounts of evidence that have come about since the original proposals of family systems theories, it is necessary to revisit, amend, and refocus our current understanding of family systems theory.

Chapter Recap

Family systems is the foundation of family therapy practice. Since people like Virginia Satir, Murray Bowen, and Salvador Minuchin proposed their ideas about family systems, there has been a surge of research regarding family relations and the processes that bind families together. But with this new research, the proposal and hypotheses of family systems theory have remained unchanged. Theory and research are supposed to have a reciprocal relationship – with new evidence, the theory changes. However, this hasn't happened with family systems theory. Current family therapy researchers often don't take the time to tie their findings to family systems theory.

This has led to family systems theory becoming unfocused. To refocus family systems theory, we need a clear definition and testable hypotheses of the theory. Family systems theory is defined as the theory that predicts and explains how people within a family interact, and how the interaction inside the family are different from those outside of it. With this definition comes the two main hypotheses. First, the family is an autonomous system. If the family is an autonomous system then the evidence would suggest that the family has rule-based, boundary-making processes that generate and maintain the family. Second, the family is an adaptable system. If the family is an adaptable system, then the evidence should suggest that the family responds to stress from inside and outside of the system by making changes to its rule-based, boundary-making processes.

Questions to Consider

1. This book proposes that family systems theory should be built on the research and proposals of biological systems. Do you agree with this assertion? What might other fields, theories, or assumptions be better suited as the foundation for family systems theory?
2. What are your thoughts on the relationship between theory and research? How can family therapy researchers and practitioners strengthen family systems theory?
3. What do you think about the description and definition of autonomy used in this chapter? How would you define it differently? Do you find it a useful concept? Or can you think of a better one?
4. What do you think about the description and definition of adaptation used in this chapter? How would you define it differently? Do you find it a useful concept? Or can you think of a better one?

Part 1

The Evidence of Autonomy and Adaptation

To better understand family systems theory, we need to understand science of the systems that are connected to the family system. Like all systems, the family system can't be understood in isolation. In the past, these systems have been referred to as "subsystems" of the family system. I've avoided using that language because each of these systems has autonomy and adapt – meaning that each of these systems, on their own, can be considered complete systems. Yet, in each system the steps or patterns in the processes that make the system autonomous and adaptable are unique. There are five systems that can help us understand and explain the family system.

The first system is the *genetic system*. Genes are the building blocks of all living systems, and this includes the family system. Evolution and genetic processes gave rise to our brains, our bodies, and our emotions – these comprise the *individual system*. This system is what helps us understand and react to people in our environment. The third system is the *attachment system* – the science of how two people connect. Because many families include more than two people, the attachment system gives rise to the *triangulation system* – the science of how three or more people connect. The attachment and triangulation systems are the patterns and processes that structure the family system. The last system that shapes the family systems science is the *sociocultural system*. This includes larger systems of power, privilege, and oppression. By understanding the science of each of these systems, and how this science is connected, we can better root our practice in evidence and potentially provide better services to our clients.

This evidence can also help us support or disprove the two hypotheses of the family systems theory. By examining the scientific evidence, we can determine whether the family is an autonomous and adaptable system and how autonomy and adaptation can cause clinical problems in families. What's more, we can use this evidence to define and describe how autonomy and adaptation operate in the family system and also discuss the things that evidence has yet to tell us about autonomy and adaptation in the family system.

Chapter 2

The Genetic and Individual Systems

Many family therapists shudder when they think about science. The word "science" brings flashbacks of statistics classes they didn't like or reading journal articles in their graduate programs. They didn't become a therapist to do science; they became therapist to help people. Clients come to therapy with deep emotional pain – they are struggling, often hurt, scared, or angry. When they come to therapy, science isn't often on their minds either. They don't want to hear therapists talk about research methods or outcomes of clinical trials; they want to be heard. They want growth. They want their pain alleviated. Yet, the scientific evidence of family systems can give therapists the tools to better conceptualize and alleviate the pain that clients experience, and it can help clients better understand their experiences.

Humans, like all animals, are the product of evolution. To understand the development of family systems and the pain clients bring to therapy, we must understand evolution and genetics. Evolution and genetic processes gave rise to our brains, our bodies, and our emotions. All of these systems are connected and shape the family system. If we want to explain the how and why of family systems theory, we must understand the current research of evolution, genetics, our brains, bodies, and emotions. These are the building blocks for the family system and the systems that produce the processes that allow the family system to maintain autonomy and adapt to the environment.

The Genetic System

Evolution is a systems idea. Evolution proposes that organisms react and respond to their environment. Their responses to the environment result in adaptations. These adaptations allow organisms to maintain their autonomy but change the ways in which the organism responds and reacts to its environment. The process of evolution through autonomy and adaptation on the earth has unfolded over more than three billion years. About 300,000 years ago the modern humans evolved and, consequently, the human family system was created. Those first family systems were different from the ones we see today, but we are still linked to those first families through genes.

Genes are the basic unit of heredity. Genes contain DNA which provides instructions on how to make proteins. Proteins perform many different functions in cells, including coordinating biological processes between cells, providing structure for cells, and binding cells together. Cells are the building blocks of life. Using proteins, they can duplicate or bond together with other cells to create tissues, organs, and bodies. The human body is made up of trillions of cells – including liver cells, skin cells, and kidney cells. Though each cell contains nearly identical genetic information, autonomy and adaptation help determine how genes are passed down through generations and how they are expressed through development.

Genes get passed down to subsequent generations through the process of natural selection. Natural selection is the most widely studied and most well-understood process of evolution. Natural selection occurs because individuals within a certain species are all genetically different from each other. Those differences affect the ability for an individual to survive and reproduce in each environment. Since those with the "good genes" in a given environment are more likely to survive and reproduce, this results in more "good genes" getting passed on. Over time, a population of a species will become more and more suited to their environment as the "good genes" spread throughout the population, and the species is more well-suited to their environment. In his 2010 book, *Why Evolution Is True*, Jerry Coyne points out a simple example:

> The wooly mammoth inhabited the parts of Eurasia and North America and was adapted to the cold by bearing a thick coat of hair (entire frozen specimens have been found buried in the tundra). It probably descended from mammoth ancestor that had little hair – like modern elephants. Mutations in the ancestral species led to some individual mammoths – like some modern humans – being hairier than others. When the climate became cold, or the species spread into more northly regions, the [hairy] individuals were better able to tolerate their frigid surroundings and left more offspring than their balder counterparts. This enriched the population in genes for hairiness. In the next generation, the average mammoth would be a bit hairier than before. Let this process continue over some thousand generations, and your smooth mammoth gets replaced by a shaggy one.
>
> (p. 11)

This process not only has occurred in mammoths, but there is evidence of natural selection in every species on the planet. In humans, we not only have evidence that natural selection shaped the physical structure of our bodies, but also have evidence that natural selection effects processes in family systems.

For example, cooperation between humans had puzzled scientists for generations. Since natural selection generally favors factors that increase the autonomy of an organism, cooperation would seem to undermine the process of natural selection. In other words, if I cooperate with you, it might mean that I must give up some of the things that I want or need to survive. However, as Coren Apicella and Joan Silk (2019) point out, natural selection may be the catalyst of humans' remarkable ability to cooperate.

For thousands of years, humans lived as hunter-gatherers. Hunter-gatherers lived in small, mobile groups that were comprised as several nuclear families. Ethnographic data from past hunter-gatherer societies as well as observation of present-day hunter-gatherer societies suggest that in many of these tribes, there was some division of labor. Some members of the group focused on gathering plant foods – which tend to have reliable returns – while others focused on hunting – which tend to have highly unreliable returns. As such, there would need to be cooperation between the gatherers and the hunters to ensure survival of the group. In addition, when a hunt was successful, the food brought back would have more food than a hunter or their immediate family could eat or store, and therefore the benefits of sharing were much higher than the risks (Apicella & Silk, 2019).

This is especially important for human reproduction. Humans have evolved a reproductive process that includes high fertility, shorter intervals between births, children who are dependent on adults for extended periods of development. This poses a problem for women and their children – women can be raising multiple children who are dependent on them for food and are calorically expensive. Studies of hunter-gatherers suggest that women produce fewer calories than they or their dependent children consume (Apicella & Silk, 2019). Therefore, for offspring to survive, hunter-gatherer tribes benefit from sharing their food with those who may or may not be genetically linked.

With this evidence, Apicella and Silk (2019) argue that cooperation in humans evolved through a process that generates "phenotypic assortment" – the environment in which hunter-gatherers lived favored those with genes that were adaptable to cultural learning, group-mindedness, and sensitivity to group norms. Over time, just like the genes for hairy mammoths, the genes for cultural learning, group-mindedness, and sensitivity to group norms were spread throughout the hunter-gatherer populations, resulting in the patterns of cooperation that are observed in family and other human social systems today.

Epigenetics

Genes are not only passed down through natural selection, but they are also expressed differently in development. As organisms grow and develop, chemical reactions take place that activate different aspects of the genome at different times. This is known as epigenetics. As Eva Jablonka and Marion Lamb described it in the 2014 book, *Evolution in Four Dimensions*:

> A person's liver cells, skins cells, and kidney cells, look different, behave differently, and function differently, yet they all contain the same genetic information. With very few exceptions, the difference between specialized cells are epigenetic, not genetic. They are consequences of events that occurred during developmental history of each cell type and determined which genes turn on, and how their products act and interact.
>
> (p. 112)

Though many cells in the human body contain the same DNA instructions, how these instructions get turned on and off depends on the epigenome. The epigenome consists of multiple chemical compounds that tell genes what to do. The compounds in the epigenome can attach themselves to DNA and turn on or off certain genes by controlling the production of proteins. The epigenome isn't changing the DNA, rather it's changing the way the cells use the DNA.

Though the epigenome doesn't change DNA, throughout development the epigenome can change. The epigenome changes in response to signals it receives. It can receive signals from inside the cell itself and from neighboring cells. For example, an embryo is made up of stem cells. Stem cells can develop into any type of cell. As an embryo develops into a baby, these stem cells receive dozens of signals from within the cell or from neighboring cells. Each signal uses the epigenome to shut down or activate certain genes to nudge the stem cells into its final type. Based on the signal the epigenome receives, a stem cell of an embryo can create a skin cell, a brain cell, or a blood cell. These differentiated cells use only 10–20% of their genes (Genetic Learning Center, 2018).

Signals within and between cells aren't the only messages the epigenome receives. The epigenome also responds and adapts to signals in an organism's environment. There is substantial evidence that exposure to trauma and/or stress can change a person's epigenome (e.g., Thayer & Kuzawa, 2011; Yehuda et al., 2015). The changes to the epigenome resulting from stress affect the development and regulation of physiological systems including the immune, cardiovascular, and stress systems (Bowers & Yehuda, 2016; Saban, Mathews, DeVon, & Janusek, 2014; Stringhini et al., 2015).

Andie Kealohi Sato Conching and Zaneta Thayer (2019) proposed a conceptual model of how the epigenome connects stress and trauma to health. Their model includes two pathways – an individual pathway and an intergenerational pathway. The individual pathway suggests that when a trauma or stressor occurs in a person's environment, it alters the epigenome. The altered epigenome modifies the expression of certain genes that then results in poorer mental and physical health.

The intergenerational pathway suggests that if a parent experiences a trauma or stressor, this can affect the offspring in multiple ways. If the parent is pregnant at the time of the trauma, the child is exposed to greater prenatal stress hormones. These stress hormones could alter the epigenome of the child. After the child is born, the trauma or stress that the parent experiences may result in different patterns of parental care. If a parent is undergoing stress, they might be at risk for mental and physical health problems which could change the way they interact with their child. The child may then be at greater risk of experiencing stress or trauma (from the parent or from the same external stressor) leading to a change in the child's epigenome. Consequently, this puts the child at a greater risk of health problems.

Epigenetic inheritance is another dimension in evolution. Genes change slowly, over multiple generations, through natural selection. The epigenome can change rapidly when responding to signals in an environment. These changes are one way that parents pass down some of their experiences to their children. Yet, the epigenome remains flexible across the lifespan and can continue to respond to changes in the environment, thereby allowing an organism to adjust its gene expression without ever changing the DNA in the genes (Genetic Learning Center, 2018).

Natural selection and epigenetic inheritance demonstrate how autonomy and adaptation occur in the genetic/cellular system. Through natural selection "good genes" get passed down across generations. "Good genes" are those that help an organism adapt to their environment. As organisms adapt, they maintain their autonomy. Natural selection happens at the genetic level, but it is also happening across time. Our epigenome allows us to adapt to the environment at the genetic level during development. As an organism gets feedback from the environment, the epigenome can turn genes on and off, allowing the organism to adapt. As the environment changes during development, the epigenome can also change, allowing the organisms to adapt so it can maintain autonomy during development.

The Individual System

Not only does autonomy and adaptation occur in the genetic system, it also occurs in the individual system. Genes and cells are the building blocks for the human body and brain. As cells combine and replicate, they give rise to systems in the body. These systems help us adapt to the environment to maintain autonomy. In particular, the nervous system has evolved as the key communicating, regulatory, and controlling system in the human body. Humans receive messages from our environment through our nervous system and our nervous systems activate our responses.

The Nervous System

The nervous system comprises the brain, the spinal cord, and the nerves that extend from the spinal cord to all other parts of the body. It is the system that connects all parts of the body together, and it plays a role in nearly every aspect of human life. The nervous system evaluates risk in the environment and matches the body's internal state to the perceived risk. When the environment is safe, the nervous system inhibits the defense structures of the brain and body. This allows for calm states to emerge. When the environment is unsafe, the nervous system can activate response to cope with threats.

The nervous system is a product of evolution. Some of the structures present in the nervous system of humans are also present in our reptilian and amphibious ancestors. Reptiles, amphibians, and mammals share two nervous system defense processes – fight-or-flight and immobilization. The fight-or-flight response allows an animal to defend itself or flee when a threat is present. Fighting or flighting requires an animal to activate the nervous system quickly and intensely, but with great cost. When the fight or flight process is activated, animals spend a lot of energy. Immobilization, on the other hand, shuts down many of the body's responses to conserve energy. This response is evolutionarily older than the fight-or-flight response (Porges, 2011).

Mammals are different from reptiles or amphibians in that they evolved a nervous system pathway to regulate these defense processes. This ability to regulate these reactions allows mammals to evolve what has been described as the social engagement system. As described by Stephen Porges (2018):

> The social engagement system enabled mammals to co-opt some of the features of the vertebrate defense systems to promote social interactions such as play and intimacy. These changes in the autonomic nervous system provided mammals with the neural mechanisms to promote biobehavioral state necessary for caring for offspring, reproducing, and cooperative behaviors.
>
> (p. 52)

In other words, some of the behaviors that are unique to mammals, especially those that help us engage socially, are evolved from the defense mechanisms. When we see a loved one, our hearts might speed up, and muscles in our face may activate. These responses use regulated versions of our fight–flight and immobilization defense processes.

The social engagement system allows mammals to signal and receive signals from others about their physiological state. The vagus nerve in the humans and other mammals has connections to multiple organs in the body, allowing them to coordinate. The vagus nerve connects to the heart, lungs, and the muscles in the face and ears, and it can modulate the tone of voice. If a person is in a state of stress their heartbeat is going to quicken. Because the heart and face muscles are connected through the vagus nerve, the state of duress will be apparent in facial expression. In addition, the connections of the vagus nerve in the inner ear can be optimized to listen for frequencies that convey social tone. If a person hears an angry tone from another person, through the connections of the vagus nerve, the tone can activate the heart and lungs, so the body can prepare itself for a negative interaction. Porges (2018) further describes the importance of these connections:

> The face-heart connection enabled mammals to detect whether a conspecific was in a calm physiological state and safe to approach, or in a highly mobilized and reactive physiological state during which engagement would be dangerous. The face-heart connection concurrently enables the individual to signal "safety" through pattern of facial expression and vocal intonation, and potentially calm an agitated conspecific to form a social relationship. When the newer mammalian vagus is optimally functioning in social interactions, emotions are well-regulated, vocal prosody is rich, and the autonomic state supports calm, spontaneous social engagement.
>
> (pp. 56–57)

Since social connection is key for mammalian survival, the evolution of the nerves in our nervous system that can react to social cues is a key adaptation. What's more, these reactions can occur outside of our consciousness. When our body reacts to social cues, we may be aware of our body's reactions, but we may not be aware of the trigger.

The Brain

Our nerves aren't the only parts of the nervous system that have evolved to read and react to social cues – our brains too have. It is estimated that more than 36 different parts of the brain are engaged to some extent or other during social interaction (Alcalá-López et al., 2018). These include structures such as the ventromedial prefrontal cortex, the cerebellum, the amygdala, the hippocampus, among many others. These structures make up many systems in the brain that coordinate social engagement. Two brain systems that are especially important to social relationships are the mirror neuron system and the mentalizing system. The mirror neuron system is what helps us learn to imitate behavior. Research suggests that the mirror neuron system activates both when we perform an action and when we observe an action being performed (Gallese, Fadiga, Fogassi, & Rizzolatti, 1996). The second system is the mentalizing system. This system allows us to attribute mental states – like thoughts, mood, intention, and emotions – to other people (Amodio & Frith, 2006). This system is activated when inner mental state of others must be inferred from their movements (Spunt & Lieberman, 2012a, 2012b).

In his 2017 article, Kai Vogeley describes how these two systems both are important in our close relationship and evolved to help us be social beings. He argues that to survive in social groups, humans need to be able to learn from and adapt to the social behavior of others. To do this successfully, we need a social detection system and a social evaluation system. Vogeley suggests that the mirror neuron system is the social detection system. This system is activated quickly and is used to process the bodily and spatial behavior of others. But we also need a social evaluation system, a system that allows us to try and make judgments about why this behavior is occurring. This is the mentalizing system. This is a "later" engaging system that allows us to evaluate relevant social information. Though one system is "early" and the other is "late," the mirror neuron and mentalization systems are complementary. "The mirror neuron system detects potentially salient social information and the mentalization system also so to determine if it is actually socially salient" (p. 8).

Researchers have tested these assertions. In their 2019 study, Alexander Geiger and his colleagues had 32 people undergo functional magnetic resonance imaging (fMRI). While doing so, they asked these people to watch video clips of people engaging in tasks while displaying certain emotions. Some were clips of people vacuuming while angry, whereas others had people painting while happy. The researcher then asked each participant to either identify the task or identify the emotion in the clip. They found that when people were asked to identify the task, the mirror neuron system was active. But when they asked the people to identify the emotion, the mentalizing system was activated. The researchers noted that:

> [B]ased on our own data we propose the complementarity of both networks in social information process according to while the mirror neuron system serves the "detection" of spatial or bodily signals such as movements, whereas mentalization system is recruited during the "evaluation" of inner experiences of others such as moods.
> (p. 202)

In other words, their findings provide evidence for Volgeley's assertions.

Emotions

Being able to detect socially relevant behavior and evaluate the meaning behind the behavior is key for survival and for creating and keeping social connections. When our brain and other parts of the nervous system detect and evaluate social cues, it usually triggers a response. These responses are known as emotions. Emotions are the way we react to the stimuli and other social cues our brain and nervous system receive. From an evolutionary perspective, emotions tells us what supports our survival and what undermines our survival (Porges, 2011). They tell us when to approach or when to run away. They help us identify who is safe and who is not. In other words, these emotions correspond with the evolution of the brain and nervous system. When our brain and nerves detect and evaluate behaviors, our emotions propel us to respond. Emotions may trigger us to shut down; they may prime us to fight or run away, or they may help us to form strong connections with others.

Jaak Panksepp (Panksepp & Biven, 2012) has focused his career on identifying emotions and their role in mammalian survival. Specifically, he coined the term "affective neuroscience" to describe his work of identifying the brain structures of emotions in mammalian brains. For emotions to be instinctual, Panksepp argues that they must produce instinctive behaviors. In other words, the emotions we feel give rise to a predictable set of psychobehavioral actions. Through his research, he has identified seven emotional systems that apply to all mammals. He capitalizes each of the systems when discussing them to differentiate them from other feelings or other reactions.

The first emotional system is SEEKING. The seeking instinct is what propels an animal to engage with its environment. Arousal of the SEEKING system allows mammals to search for and acquire resources that are needed for survival. As described by George Ellis and Mark Solms (2018):

> Typical mammalian SEEKING behaviors are foraging and similar generalized exploratory activities (imagine a dog in an open field). An interesting and important fact about the SEEKING system is tis primary "objectless" quality. It does not drive the animal to seek specific objects in response to specific needs . . . it motivates the animal to go out and explore, to look for something – anything – interesting and nice. It propels the animal to investigate the world and engage with it, in the firm belief that whatever it needs or wants, it is "out there."
> (p. 89)

The SEEKING system is not about trying to find something in particular, but it can lead to learning. If an animal goes out and explores and finds something that can meet a particular need, the animal can create connections. The animal can learn that when a certain need is activated, it can go out and find the same thing it found before (Panksepp & Biven, 2012.) The SEEKING system also keeps us motivated when we face adversity. For example, when we are hungry, cold, or thirsty, the SEEKING system motivates us to continue to find the resources we need (Panksepp & Biven, 2012).

The second emotional system is LUST (Panksepp & Biven, 2012). As with other instinctual emotional systems, the LUST system produces instinctive behaviors. When the LUST system is active behaviors ranging from courting, to copulation, to orgasm occur. The LUST system is key to survival as it allows animals to identify a mate and reproduce. In addition, Panksepp and Biven argue that LUST is not just about reproduction and future generations, but about promoting the health and longevity of a pair-bond.

> A satisfying sex life promotes a competent immune system and longevity, just as physical exercise does. Although sexual gratification may not be an immediate aid to survival, well-bonded, sexually satisfied people often live longer than those without the security of happy relationships, whether their parings be man with woman, man with man, or woman with woman.
>
> (p. 247)

LUST, then, is key to the survival of future generations not only by passing on genes but also by bonding pairs together, improving their health and creating a sense of security.

The third system is RAGE. The role of this instinctual emotional system is competing for and defending resources (Davis & Montag, 2019). In addition, circumstances such as irritation or restricting movement can evoke the RAGE system. As with other systems, the RAGE system results in behaviors. Again, Ellis and Solms (2018):

> Like all the other instincts, activation of this emotional system evokes a particular set of behaviors. In this case, full-blown "affective attack" behaviors including baring the teeth, raising the forelimbs, extending the claws (if you have them), piloerection, and lunging towards the object of your wrath. More muted anger behaviors include, for instance, pacing and growling. Such behaviors are always guided and accompanied by particular feeling states – in this case, feelings of irritability, anger, or outright rage.
>
> (p. 92)

It is important to distinguish the RAGE system from other systems. When a predator is hunting prey, it is activating the SEEKING system, not the

RAGE system – it is hungry, not angry. If the predator needs to defend its catch from others, it may activate the RAGE system to fight off anything that might try to steal it (Panksepp & Biven, 2012).

The fourth system is the FEAR system. The FEAR system is commonly referred to as the fight-or-flight responses. The fight-or-flight behavioral responses are accompanied by feelings of anxiety, fear, or trepidation. As with other instinctual emotions, these feelings are manifest in physiological changes such as shallow breathing, increased heart rate, and redirection of blood flow. Some aspects of fear are learned. We can learn to associate objects, other species, or are conspecifics with FEAR. But some are passed through evolution. For example, newborn mice which have never been exposed to cats still elicit fear responses when coming into contact with cat hair (Ellis & Solms, 2018).

The fifth system is PANIC/GRIEF. This system can also be described as the "attachment" instinct. When an animal first experiences a separation from an attachment figure, it experiences panic. If that animal doesn't reconnect with that attachment figure, the panic gives way to grief. All mammals display panic when being separated from an attachment figure. This is known as protest behavior. When mammals protest, they emit distress vocalization, and they search anxiously for the attachment figure. If they don't find the attachment figure, mammals transition from protest to despair. The mammal will start displaying behavior associated with sadness – sluggishness and crying. These feelings of sadness and panic are the evolutionary price mammals pay for the biological advantage of attachment (Ellis & Solms, 2018).

The sixth system is CARE. This system can also be viewed as an attachment system. Instead of focusing on panic/grief of a loss or separation of an attachment figure, this system initiates nurturant behaviors (Davis & Montag, 2019). For example, if a baby is crying, mammals engage in soothing behaviors – touch or soft vocalizations. Panksepp and Bivin (2012) argue that these behaviors are innate and the nurturant behaviors that mammals engage in don't have to be learned through observation.

The final system is PLAY. The PLAY system is especially strong among young mammals and engages them in activities like chasing, wrestling, or running. The PLAY system helps mammals socially bond and learn social limits (Davis & Montag, 2019). As Ellis and Solms suggest:

> [PLAY] is about finding the limits of what is socially appropriate, tolerable, acceptable, permissible. When play is no longer fun for one of the participants, they don't do it anymore. The limit has been reached... [PLAY results in] the establishment of social hierarchies – of a "pecking order." Accordingly, juvenile rough an tumble play increasingly give way to competitive games, and also (in humans) to "pretend" play, in which participant try out social roles.... We do

not know what goes on in the imagination of other mammals when they do play, but we would confidently suggest that they too are "trying out" different social roles, and learning what they can get away with.

(pp. 98–99)

Social play can result in the development of rules. As mammals engage in play, reach the boundaries, and respond accordingly, rules of social behavior get enacted. These rules then serve to regulate social behavior and protect mammals from excesses of their instinct (Ellis & Solms, 2018).

In their book, Panksepp and Bivin (2012) outline the key brain structures associated with each of these emotion systems, noting however that many of these emotional systems have overlapping controls. As such, multiple systems can be activated at a time. For example, we may be out seeking or exploring our world, and then experience rage when our efforts are thwarted. Or we may experience lust toward a potential mate and also experience panic that this potential mate might not reciprocate those feelings.

The nervous system and emotional systems demonstrate how autonomy and adaptation occur at an individual level. Humans receive signal from their environment, this triggers physiological responses and psychobehavioral behaviors. The responses and behaviors help an individual adapt to their environment to maintain autonomy. These responses and behaviors may change during development as a person learns and can make predictions about their environment, but they are also the product of evolution. Generations of mammalian evolution have resulted in these responses and behaviors.

Emotion Regulation

However, humans aren't governed only by instinct. We are also able to monitor and inhibit some of our reactions. We have evolved other brain structures that give us the ability to regulate our emotions. Emotion regulation allows us to pursue goals that may not be in line with the emotion reaction we are experiencing. In some instances, we may want to decrease our emotions – we may want to tamp down our anger in a public space; or we may want to increase our emotions – sharing positive news with a loved one. As James Gross (2013) describes it:

> Motives for up-regulating negative emotions include promoting a focused, analytic mindset; fostering an empathetic stance; and influencing others' actions. Motived got down regulating positive

emotions include maintaining a realistic mindset; being mindful of social conventions; and concealing one's feelings from others.

(p. 9)

Humans' ability to regulate their emotions allows them to better connect with others, but also allows them to pursue goal-directed behavior.

A model of emotion regulation was proposed by Jennifer Yih and her colleagues in 2019. They suggested that current research on emotion and emotion regulation suggests that these processes can be viewed as a loop – a WPVA loop. They write:

> Emotion generation and emotion regulation can be viewed as a cybernetic control processes that, based on perceptual input, output actions for approach a target state. Such process interface with the world (W) by perceiving some aspects of it (P), evaluating these aspects in relation to valued goals (V) and initiating actions (A) to bring the world closer to those goals. WPVA loop operate iteratively to enable an individual to adaptively respond to changing goals and environment.
>
> (p. 43)

WPVA loops occur both for emotions and for the emotion regulation process. A WPVA *emotion loop* occurs when we monitor the environment, see a potential significant stimulus, appraise it, and activate one or many of our emotional systems. A WPVA *emotion regulation loop* occurs in response to emotion system activation. When we recognize the emotion system being activated, we attend to it, evaluate if and how it should be regulated, and initiate a strategy to regulate it.

Researchers have also begun exploring specific emotion regulation strategies to uncover what is "good" or "bad" emotion regulation. When studying emotion regulation strategies, six strategies are often examined: *acceptance* – a non-judgmental stance where emotions are acknowledged in the present and accepted for what they are; *avoidance* – emotions are ignored or downplayed; *problem-solving* – attempts to change or contain a stressful emotional situation through specific actions; *reappraisal* – creating positive or neutral interpretations of emotional experiences; *rumination* – repetitively focusing on an emotional experience or situation; and *suppression* – concealing or squashing an emotional reaction.

These six emotion regulation strategies have a large impact on mental health. In adults, avoidance, rumination, and suppression are strongly associated with depression and anxiety symptoms while acceptance, problem-solving, and reappraisal are associated with lower levels of depression and anxiety (Aldao, Nolen-Hoeksema, & Schweizer, 2010).

In adolescents, the same patterns exist, but in some cases the associations are stronger (Schäfer, Naumann, Holmes, Tuschen-Caffier, & Samson, 2017).

Emotion regulation loops and emotion regulation strategies allow humans greater flexibility to meet goals. For example, if a person is perceiving a potentially dangerous event occurring in their environment, they may activate their FEAR system. Their heart rate might increase, pumping more blood to places that can help them fight or flee. Once this WVAP loop for emotion is activated, the WVAP regulation loop may then begin. If the fear-activating situation is that the person must speak before a large audience, then it would be important for that person to activate strategies that can downregulate their FEAR system to allow them to give their presentation. They may try to suppress their fear response to try and calm down, or they may try to accept it. If a person feels threatened by a loved one by a breakup or divorce, this may activate the PANIC/GRIEF response. This again will result in changes to the body and the person may try to avoid their emotions by pretending they are "fine" with the situation; they may ruminate and obsess about the loss of the loved one; or they may try to problem solve and find a way to either move forward or try to reconcile.

Chapter Recap

The genetic and individual systems are two of the core systems that create the family system. These systems are the product of evolution. Genes get passed down through the generations through natural selection. Natural selection occurs because organisms are genetically different from each other. Those who are better suited to their environment are more likely to survive and reproduce – there genes are more likely to get passed on. Evolution through natural selection has not only resulted in the structure of our human bodies and brains but also helped give rise to human's ability to socialize in groups. Natural selection isn't the only way that our genes are shaped, they can also be expressed differently in development. This happens because of the epigenome. The epigenome receives signal from the environment and from neighboring cells and can change the expression of genes based on these signals. Stress can change the epigenome, making the brain and body more susceptible to disease and other problems.

Natural selection and epigenetic inheritance show how autonomy and adaptation occur in the genetic system. Through natural selection, genes that help an organism survive get passed to offspring, because those with these genes are more likely to reproduce. In addition, our epigenome allows us to adapt to the environment. As an organism gets feedback from the environment, the epigenome can turn genes on and off, allowing the organism to adapt. As the environment changes during development, the epigenome can also change, allowing the organisms to adapt so it can maintain autonomy during development.

Genes and the epigenome are the building blocks for the individual system. The nervous system – the brain, the spinal cord, and the nerves that extend from it – is a key component that allows individuals to adapt and maintain autonomy. The nervous system receives signals from the environment and is responsible for activating our responses. The nervous system is responsible for our fight, flight, or freeze, but it has also evolved to help us engage socially. This social engagement is key to human survival – to survive in groups we need to be able to read and respond to social cues.

The brain, as a part of the nervous system, also evolved to help us read and react to social cues. The brain has two key systems that help us understand social cues – the mirror neuron system and the mentalizing system. These systems allow us to detect social cues and evaluate them. Being able to detect socially relevant behavior and evaluate the meaning behind the behavior is key for survival and for creating and keeping social connections. When our brain and other parts of the nervous system detect and evaluate social cues, it usually triggers a response. These responses are known as emotions. Emotions are the way we react to the stimuli and other social cues our brain and nervous system receive.

The brain has seven key emotion systems – SEEKING, LUST, RAGE, FEAR, PANIC/GRIEF, CARE, and PLAY. These systems help us stay close to important others, engage with our environment, and defend or run away when things are not safe. When humans receive signal from their environment, this triggers physiological responses and psychobehavioral behaviors. The responses and behaviors help individuals adapt to their environment to maintain autonomy. However, humans don't just react, they can also regulate their emotions. Regulating emotions allows us to connect with others and pursue goal-directed behavior. But when done poorly, emotion regulation can lead to problematic behavior and emotional responses.

Questions to Consider

1. This chapter argued that evolution is important to the family system, and the family system is a product of evolution. What are your opinions on this assertion? What are the benefits and limitations of evolutionary explanations of human behavior?
2. What is your reaction to the suggestion of Coren Apicella and Joan Silk that cooperation is a product of evolution? Do you

agree with the assertion that cooperation that we see today resulted from hunter-gatherer societies needed to share food and other resources?
3. What do you think about the research and assertions put forth by Stephen Porges? He argues that the vagus nerve connects multiple parts of the body, gives humans and other mammals the ability to read and respond to social cues.
4. Jaak Panksepp proposed seven emotional systems. How do these systems affect the family system? How do these emotion systems underlie patterned behavior in the family system?

Chapter 3

The Attachment, Triangulation, and Family Systems

When a child is born, genes, an epigenome, a brain, and the nervous system are typically present. They are ready to be signaled by the outside world and to react to it. The child has all the physical systems it needs to be autonomous. However, this child is wholly dependent on others for its survival – without caretakers, the child dies. To survive, the child must connect with other people.

The connections made between children and caregivers, partners, siblings, in-laws, and other relatives are the processes that generate and sustain the family system. Without the connections, there is no system. The interactions that create and sustain the connections are necessary for the family system to be autonomous. Yet these connections, by definition, are adaptations. When we connect, we must react and respond to the person(s) we are connecting with. These reactions are the adaptations that serve to maintain the autonomy of the individual and the autonomy and relationship. But without an adaptation, there is no relationship.

In the family system, there can be many types of connections. Let us start out by exploring dyadic connections – including parent–child and romantic partner relationships. These dyadic relationships are all part of the attachment system.

The Attachment System

For decades, Ed Tronick and his colleagues have been conducting what is known as the Still-Face experiment (e.g., Tronick, Als, Adamson, Wise, & Brazelton, 1978; Weinberg & Tronick, 1996; Dicorcia, Snidman, Sravish, & Tronick, 2016). In these experiments, babies from ages 1 to 2 and their mothers sit down and begin to interact. The mother smiles and is responsive to the baby; they laugh together, and they coordinate their emotions.

Then the mother begins not to respond to the baby – the mother only shows a "still face." The baby quickly notices the change in the mother and begins reacting to the change in the mother. The baby may smile at the mother; it may point to things around the room, but the mother is non-responsive. The baby is trying to do everything it can to get the mother to reengage. After the mother fails to respond to the baby's attempts to engage, the baby becomes dysregulated. The baby may begin to reach for the mother, make distressing sounds, until finally the baby melts down. The baby becomes overwhelmed and cries. The mother then reengages with the baby, and the baby calms down. They begin to play, smile, connect, and laugh.

The Still-Face experiment and others like it (e.g., the Strange Situation Experiment) are part of the growing body of evidence supporting attachment theory. Attachment theory was developed by John Bowlby and Mary Ainsworth. Their work throughout the mid-twentieth century laid the foundation for the myriad of attachment studies we have today. Though much research has been devoted to explaining attachment "styles" – an individual's manner of attaching, there is evidence that an attachment "style" may be relationship dependent – more of a system than a style. Individuals may form a secure relationship system with one person but may form an insecure attachment system with another person.

In a study of adolescents, Anna Beth Doyle and her colleagues (2009) suggested that "attachment styles varied strikingly between attachment figures" (p. 706) – teenagers showed different attachment "styles" depending on which relationship they were discussing. In addition, research also suggests that the attachment system between a mother and a child isn't associated with the attachment system of that same child and its father (George, Cummings, & Davies, 2010; Benware, 2013) – a child doesn't have an attachment style, they are embedded into a dyadic attachment system. Though the systems may be different, the process of the attachment system follows similar steps.

Researcher and couple therapy innovator, Sue Johnson, suggests that interactions in the attachment system have five basic moves. First, we *reach* out to others and invite connection. If we connect with the others we are reaching for, we can more easily regulate our emotions and calm our nervous system. If our reaching isn't responded to, we then either *protest and push* for more connection or *turn away and shut down*. If pushing for connection or turning away doesn't result in connection, we go into *melt down* – we may get angry, scared, or sad. Finally, if we have a good relationship, we find a way to *reconnect*.

In their book, *Attachment in Adulthood*, Mario Mikulincer and Phillip Shaver (2007) described how this process promotes a sense of self.

> This cycle – experiencing threats or distress, seeking protection and comfort from an attachment figure, experiencing stress reduction and felt security, and returning to other interests and activities – provides

a prototype of both successful emotion regulation and regulation of interpersonal closeness. Knowing that coping with threats and distress is possible (through affection, gaining assistance, solving pressing problems) gives a person a script for regulating negative emotions, maintaining equanimity, and sustaining valuable relationships ... When one is suffering or worried it is useful to seek comfort from other; when suffering is alleviated, it is possible to engage in other activities and entertain other priorities. When attachment relationships function well, a person learns that distance and autonomy are completely compatible with closeness and reliance on other.

(p. 13)

Like Sue Johnson, Mikulincer and Shaver argue that disconnection that leads to reconnection, strengthens not only relationships but also allows for individuality. If we can trust that someone will be there for us when we are stressed, we are more likely to explore and be independent.

Parenting

Looking at the interaction in the Still-Face experiment, we can see the steps in the parent–child attachment system. When the mother's face goes still, the child reaches to reestablish the connection. As the mother's face remains still, the child protests and pushes for more connection. This doesn't work, so the child melts down and begins to cry. When the mother reengages, the child calms down and is able to go back to laughing and connecting with the mother.

These findings are supported by other research on parenting conducted by developmental psychologist Diana Baumrind (1966, 2013). Baumrind is known for her work on parenting styles, but the dimensions of her parenting styles – demandingness and responsiveness – highlight the process of the attachment system and autonomy and adaptation.

Baumrind suggests:

> *Responsiveness* refers to parents' emotional warmth and supportive action that are attuned to children's vulnerabilities, cognitions, and inputs and are supportive of children's individual needs and plans. *Demandingness* has two related components, monitoring and confrontive control, and refers to the claims parents make on their children to become integrated into and contribute to the family unit: *monitoring* which provides structure, order, and predictability to the child's life; and *control*, which shapes the child's behavior restrains the child's potentially disruptive agentic expressions.
>
> (p. 26)

These two dimensions are independent factors – parents who are highly responsive can also be highly demanding. Further, Baumrind suggests that good parenting is not about finding a balance between responsiveness and demandingness. Rather, optimal parenting, she argues, occurs when parents have a combination of firm control and are highly emotional responsive to their children's needs.

Research has tended to support these assumptions. Meta-analytic studies have found that parents who exhibit high levels of responsiveness and set firm boundaries have children who display fewer internalizing and externalizing symptoms; and for children with internalizing or externalizing disorders, being responsive as a parent and setting firm boundaries is associated with a symptom decrease over time. On the other hand, parents who use harsh control or who are neglectful have children with higher levels of internalizing and externalizing symptoms and these symptoms tend to get worse over time (Pinquart, 2016, 2017). Similar results have been found for delinquency (Hoeve et al., 2009) and aggression (Kawabata, Alink, Tseng, Ijzendoorn, & Crick, 2011). In other words, when the parent–child attachment system is responsive, safe, and predictable, children develop a sense of individuality and are better able to regulate their emotions.

Couples

The steps of the attachment system are also visible in romantic partnerships. Often labeled a demand–withdraw pattern, extensive research has observed attachment interactions in couples (Schrodt, Witt, & Shimkowski, 2014). The research focuses on the *protest and push* or the *turn away and shut down* steps in the attachment system. For example, Laren Papp and her colleagues (2009) had 116 couples keep diary reports of the marital conflict. They found that when couples were discussing issues relating to their own relationship (when compared to issues such as children, friends, or other events) they were more likely to demonstrate demand–withdraw behavior. They also found that after being in a demand–withdraw pattern, couples were also likely to try and reconnect by apologizing. In other words, couples were reaching, not getting the response they hoped for, either protesting or shutting down, but then finding ways to connect again.

When couples aren't able to reconnect following a *protest–push/turn away–shut down* interactions, they can get stuck in destructive patterns of behavior. Sue Johnson (2019) describes four such patterns. The first, and the most common, is the *criticize–withdraw* cycle. In this cycle, one person is protesting their disconnection – with anger and blame – while the other is pulling back and shutting down. The second is the *attack–attack* cycle. This cycle is relatively short. The goal of this cycle is to "define the other as at fault [to create] an illusionary moment of control in the wave of distress that engulfs a . . . relationship" (p. 138). The third is the *freeze and flee* cycle. People in this cycle are burnt out, discouraged, and at risk of ending their connection. Instead of reaching for connection they may avoid each other. Finally, there is the *chaos and ambivalence* cycle. In this cycle one person may demand closeness, but when it is offered by the other, "the threat involved in being vulnerable with a needed other triggers reactive defense and distance, which then pushes the other partner into frustrated withdrawal" (p. 138).

Another important aspect of the romantic partner attachment system is sexual intimacy. Sexual physical intimacy can bond partners together – when partners engage in sexual activity the body gets increased exposure to oxytocin – a neuropeptide that promotes bonding. Sex promotes bonding, but a healthy attachment system also promotes better sex. As Guit Birnhaum and Harry Reis (2019) suggest:

> Smooth functioning of the attachment system encourages self-assured approach to sexuality, ease with sexual intimacy, and enjoyment of mutual sexual interactions within the context of committed relationships. In particular, people who are secure with respect to attachment tend to engage in sex mainly to intensify the relationship with the current partner . . . Overall, the confident approach to sexuality that comes with attachment security promotes pleasurable engagement in affectionate and exploratory sexual activities, thereby fostering relationship quality and longevity.
>
> (p. 12)

Sex is, for many couples, an important part of the romantic partner attachment system. A healthy attachment system promotes a healthy sexual relationship, and healthy sexual relationship promotes a healthy attachment system.

A key aspect of a healthy sexual system is desire. Though desire tends to ebb and flow across the duration of partnership (Acevedo & Aron, 2009), research suggests that certain factors can promote a healthy sexual system. Kristen Mark and Julie Lasslo (2018) reviewed 64 studies to develop a conceptual model of maintaining desire in long-term relationships. At the core of this model were the ideas of individuality and the attachment system. They noted that "maintaining a level of autonomy in a relationship and being able to continue to have an identity that is separate from the couple identity has been shown to contribute to the maintenance of sexual desire" (pp. 568–569). In addition, they noted how research has supported the idea that an attachment system that is responsive and emotionally supportive is also key to sexual desire.

These finding echo the ideas of noted couple therapist Esther Perel. Perel (2013) suggests:

> At the heart of sustaining desire in a committed relationship . . . is the reconciliation of two fundamental human needs. On the one hand, our need of security, for predictability, for safety, for dependability, for reliability, for permanence. All these anchoring, grounding experiences of our lives that we call home. But we also have an equally strong need . . . for adventure, for novelty, for mystery, for risk, for danger, for the unknown, for the unexpected surprise . . . In this dilemma about reconciling two sets of fundamental needs, there are a few things that erotic couples do. One, they have a lot of sexual privacy. They understand that there is an erotic space that belongs to each of them. . . [Two], erotic couples also understand that passion waxes and wanes . . . But they know how to resurrect it . . . they understand that . . . committed sex is premeditated sex. It's willful. It's intentional. It's focus and presence.

Perel is highlighting the sexual system's need for individuality and flexibility. Partners need their own erotic space and they also need to allow their desire and eroticism to grow and adapt to the ebbs and flows of desire. When the sexual system fails to adapt to the ebbs and flows of life, or when partners shut down or disown their sexual desire, the sexual system becomes problematic.

The Attachment System and the Genetic and Individual System

The attachment system is a core process of binding together individuals within a family system – forming an attachment system is necessary for survival. But the attachment system doesn't exist in isolation. Marije Verhage and her colleagues (2016) found that the sensitivity and responsiveness between parents and children explain only about 50% of the association between parent and child. In other words, a child's attachment system is not solely dependent on the responsiveness of the parent. Nor is the attachment system of partners solely dependent on the responsiveness of the other partner. The attachment system is embedded in the genetic and individual systems of the people in that system.

In a review of attachment research, Lisa Golds and her colleagues (2020) sought to understand how the effects of genetics on attachment may be influenced by the environmental systems the child is in. They examined 27 studies that had examined the interactions of genes, environment, and attachment. They found little evidence to support specific genes were linked to specific attachment system patterns (secure, insecure, disorganized) – genes don't cause an attachment style; however, they did find evidence to support the idea that "genes work in a regulated way to moderate behavior depending on the attachment classification that the child represents, and the environment which the child finds himself or herself" (p. 20). In other words, the attachment system influences and is influenced by the genetic and other environmental systems of the child. The attachment system adapts to signals that it receives from these other systems, shaping itself to the given context.

Autonomy and adaptation are key features of attachment system. Attachment systems that are responsive, safe, and predictable can maintain their autonomy – generate connections, be sustained across time and during stress. But these attachment systems can also adapt to the current environment – create a safe space during stress and allow people to explore when things are calm. When attachment systems are non-responsive and unsafe, this can lead to a breakdown of the system. Marriages that have harmful attachment processes may be more likely to break up (McNelis & Segrin, 2019), and the individuals within those distressed marriages are at greater risk for mental and physical health problems (Roberson, Shorter, Woods, & Priest, 2018; Whisman, 2007) and can put greater stress on their nervous system (Priest, Roberson, & Woods, 2019). Children in attachment systems that are unsafe and unresponsive also have similar risks (Widom, Czaja, Kozakowski, & Chauhan, 2018).

The Triangulation System

Though the attachment system is an important system, it rarely exists in isolation. Most people find themselves in multiple attachment systems. A person may have an attachment to a parent, a romantic partner, children, and other important people in their life. These attachment systems influence and are influenced by each other. They may be replicated – people who had safe parent–child attachment systems growing up are more likely to develop safe romantic attachments in adulthood – but they also can be dynamic – the introduction of a child into a safe romantic attachment can destabilize or stress that attachment system. The interacting attachment systems and the dynamic interplay between them can often create triangles. Triangles are created to stabilize or to reinforce attachment systems.

As defined by Rudi Dallos and Arlene Vetere (2012), triangulation is "the idea that what is happening in a significant relationship between two people in a family can have a powerful influence on a third family member, and vice versa, in mutually reinforcing ways" (p. 119).

Triangles can be created in many ways, but research has explored some common examples of how triangulation processes occur and how autonomy and adaptation drive this system.

The Parent–Child Triangle

One of the most common triangulation systems that occur in families is between two parents and a child. There are many ways in which this triangulation system can arise in the family, but it typically follows a pattern (Dallos & Vetere, 2012). At the center of this triangulation system is a stressed romantic partnership. As stress arises and is unresolved between partners, a child begins to monitor this stress. As the child monitors the stress, the child may become dysregulated. As it becomes dysregulated, the child may begin to engage in a behavior that show this dysregulation. As the parents notice this dysregulation, they can begin to focus on the child. The focus on the child allows the parents to displace the stress from their relationship into the child's behavior. Though this behavior stabilizes the parent's relationship, it doesn't address the underlying stress in that relationship. This increases the child's dysregulation, exacerbates the child's behavior, and allows the parents to put even more energy into solving the child's issue.

Rudi Dallos and Arlene Vetere (2012) provide an example of how this pattern can develop even at a young age:

> Two parents are discussing an issue that arouses anxiety and one or both begin to show signs of discomfort. The young child, playing in the room, gets up and toddles over to one parent, who with some relief, bends down, pick up the child, puts them on their lap and pats them, and so on. And thus, the difficult adult conversation is interrupted, unhelpful arousal is calmed by the action of attending to and soothing the child and the child learns, before they can even use language, how they can be helpful to their parents. If this sequence is repeated and positively reinforced a few times it could become established as a pattern or a set of expectations about how to manage unhelpful arousal.
>
> (pp. 119–120)

This type of process can be replicated throughout the lifespan. There may be stress in a romantic partnership which a teenager might monitor. Instead of approaching the parents, the dysregulated teen may begin to do poorly at school, requiring the parents to focus their attention on the teen's school performance and not addressing the underlying tension in the romantic partner system.

Research has repeatedly shown evidence for distressed romantic partnerships leading to parent–child triangles and that triangulation can have problematic effects for kids and teens. Gregory Fosco and John Grych (2010) studied 171 teenagers aged 14–19 at two time points and found that teens who reported higher levels of conflict between their parents had the highest levels of triangulation – findings that had been previously found by others (e.g., Grych, Raynor, & Fosco, 2004). In addition, Fosco and Grych found that those teens who felt caught in the middle of their parents' stress reported higher levels of self-blame and had poorer relationships with their parents – these findings were similar for both boys and girls and for those in intact and divorced families. The parent–child triangle has also been linked to internalizing (Buehler & Welsh, 2009) and externalizing (Fosco, Lippold, & Feinberg, 2014) in adolescents.

Other research on triangulation have also identified individual system factors that increase the risk of the parent–child triangle and children's reactions to being triangulated. When children are triangulated, research suggests that they usually respond in two ways. Again, Dallos and Vetere (2012) summarize this, suggesting:

> One [strategy] is to try and avoid the conflicts between their parents by escaping, retreating to their room, staying out of the home as much as possible and disconnecting emotionally. The other is to attempt to intervene, for example, to keep the peace, reason with the parent to stop, and try to be particularly nice and pleasant. It also seems that some children may intervene with their own arousal regulation problems by . . . shouting at their parents, becoming hostile and getting into trouble. These can be even more successful ways of distracting their parents so the child, not their parents' relationship, comes to be seen as the problem, as negative interaction cycles escalate.
>
> (p. 125)

Parents with lots of conflict, the presence of a depressed parent, and a child with poor emotion regulation are all risk factors of a child to respond in these two ways. In some instances, these processes do not end in childhood or adolescent; they continue into adulthood (Amato & Afifi, 2006).

The Infidelity Triangle

Another common triangle is the infidelity triangle. Infidelity can come in various constellations – emotional infidelity, sexual infidelity, or combinations of both (Blow & Hartnett, 2005). What's more, developments in technology have allowed infidelity to exist digitally. However, as Ester Perel (2017) notes, infidelity typically includes one or more of three things – secrecy, sexual alchemy, and emotional involvement.

Secrecy is "the number one organizing principle of an infidelity. An affair always lives in the shadow of the primary relationship, hoping never to be discovered" (Perel, 2017, p. 24). Perel prefers the term sexual alchemy to "sex" because it doesn't mean that infidelity must be contained to specific sexual acts. "Affairs sometimes involve sex, sometimes not, but they are always erotic . . . the kiss we imagine giving can be as powerful and exciting as hours of actual lovemaking" (p. 26). Emotional involvement in infidelity can vary wildly. On the one end there can be a love affair – where people are connected to what they may deem the "love of their life." On the other end there can be affairs that lack emotion such as recreation, anonymous, or paid sexual encounters (Perel, 2017). Each of these components of infidelity is in place to one degree or another when an affair occurs and can have strong impacts on couples and families. Research has begun to tease out how the infidelity triangle can develop and effect romantic partnership.

Because there can be various types of affairs, it is hard to study the frequency of infidelity in relationships. Most research on infidelity only explores extramarital sex, as it is easier to define and measure. When defined as just extramarital sex, about 1.5–5% of partners will have extramarital sex each year, while 22–25% of men and 11–13% of women will have extramarital sex in their lifetime (Labrecque & Whisman, 2017). In their review of research on this type infidelity, Frank Fincham and Ross May described individual and relationship factors that increase the likelihood of infidelity. Individuals who had higher levels of narcissism, had previously engaged in infidelity, had problematic substance use, and/or had greater psychological distress were more likely to have an affair. Romantic relationships that had low satisfaction, low commitment, had similar levels of education, the same religious beliefs, and had cohabitated before marriage also had a greater risk for infidelity.

Though researchers have looked at risk factors of infidelity, less is known about the process. Gurit Birnbaum and her colleagues (2019) explored the process of infidelity – examining how partners turn to others outside their relationship. In a series of four studies, these researchers found that a person who reports higher levels of relationship conflict and less desire for their partner were more likely to approach potential alternative mates and more likely to flirt with attractive strangers. Birnbaum and her colleagues concluded that "partner's hurtful behavior diminishes the desire for these partners, directing attention, at least momentarily, to new seemingly more promising relationships" (p. 712).

Romantic relationships may be at even greater risk if the person one partner is turning toward is a close friend. In their 2019 study, Lindsay Labrecque and Mark Whisman examined the association between having extramarital sex and marital dissolution. Using a sample of 1,853 married adults, they explored whether having an affair was associated with divorce two years later and if this association changes depending on who the extramarital partner was. Compared to those who didn't have a sexual affair, those who did were five times more likely to divorce.

Those who had extramarital sex with a close friend were seven times more likely to divorce than those who did not have extramarital sex. In other words, having an affair increases the likelihood of divorce, but having an affair with a close friend further increases that risk.

Autonomy and Adaptation in Triangulation Systems

The processes of the parent–child and infidelity triangle and the research supporting them show how this triangulation system is rooted in autonomy and adaptation. Stress in the romantic partnership threatens the generation and maintenance of the attachment system. To try and stabilize the partner attachment system, the system must adapt. One way to adapt is to triangulate a child or an extramarital partner into the stress. If a child is brought into the stress, the child must adapt in response to the pressure – the child may begin to act or shut down. This results in a cycle of increased pressure on the child resulting in more problematic behavior. The more stressed the child becomes the less pressure is on the partner attachment system, ensuring its autonomy. If an extramarital partner is brought in, instead of potentially stabilizing the romantic partnership, it may lead to more conflict between partners and eventual breakup. When a dyadic relationship is under stress, a triangle is created to help the relationship adapt to the pressure but often results in negative outcomes.

The parent–child and the infidelity triangles, though common, are not the only way triangulation occurs. Michael Kerr and Murry Bowen (1988) suggested at least four ways in which triangles can be created or destabilized. First, as shown in the parent–child triangle, an unstable dyadic relationship can be stabilized by the addition of a third person. Second, an unstable dyad can be stabilized by removing a third person. This can occur through emotional cutoff. If two people can exile another person through their mutual dislike of that person, their relationship becomes more stable. Third, the addition of a third person can destabilize a previous stable dyad. This is evident in the infidelity triangle. If an extramarital affair occurs, the couple is more likely to end their relationship. Finally, a stable dyadic relationship can become unstable by the removal of a third person. For example, when a child leaves home for college, marital conflict might increase.

A triangle may be an adaptation – it forms in response to stress within or outside the family system. Yet, it can also be an autonomy sustaining process – the interaction between three or more people may bind the system together. In addition, triangulation is not always negative. Though most research on triangulation has focused on maladaptive triangles and the negative outcomes associated with these triangles, triangles can be a positive sustaining process or a positive adaptation. If two partners decide to have a child, the entry of that child into the system does not mean that the relationship between the partners will destabilize. The choice to have a child may further bond the partners together and strengthen their commitment to each other, which may in turn increase their relationship satisfaction.

The Family System

The attachment and triangulation systems create the processes that structure the family system. These interlocking and overlapping systems give rise to autonomy and adaptation at the family level. If a family system consists of attachment systems that are responsive and safe and has triangulation systems that serve to promote connection and individuality of the individuals in the system, then it is likely that the family system will have processes that promote autonomy yet allow the system to adapt – the family will be cohesive and flexible. If the family system has unresponsive and unpredictable attachment systems and triangulation systems that are used to alienate a family member or avoid conflict, these family systems are likely to have problems with autonomy and adaptation – they may lack connection or may not be flexible. Research using David Olson's Circumplex Model has begun to map and describe how the attachment and triangulation systems and the processes within those systems give rise to family system dynamics (Olson, Waldvogel, & Schilieff, 2019).

The Circumplex Model asserts that there are three important dimensions in family system functioning. The first is cohesion. Olson defines cohesion as, "the emotional bonding that a couple and family members have toward one another . . . Cohesion focuses on how systems balance separateness and togetherness" (p. 201). Cohesion reflects the autonomy-making processes of the family system. In families with healthy cohesion, individuals within the family not only are able to have independence but also can stay connected to other members of the family. Families with problematic cohesion are often enmeshed – high emotional connection with little autonomy – or disengaged – high levels of independence with little emotional connection to the family.

The second dimension is flexibility. Olson defines flexibility as "the amount of change in [family] leadership, role relationships, and relationships rules . . . Flexibility focuses on how systems balance stability with change" (p. 202). Flexibility is the adaptive process in the family system. Families with healthy flexibility can balance change and stability in functional ways. Problematic flexibility can occur when a family is too flexible with little structure – Olson calls this chaotic, or it can occur when a family isn't flexibly enough – Olson calls this rigid.

The third is communication. Communication is viewed as the dimension that facilitates cohesion and flexibility in the family. "Good communication helps couples and families alter their levels of cohesion and flexibility to better deal with developmental or situation demands" (p. 202). Family with good communication can listen to each other, share their emotions, and show respect for each other. Families with poor communication will often blame each other, become defensive, and self-disclose inappropriately or not at all.

One of the key assumptions of the Circumplex Model is the balance hypothesis. This hypothesis suggests that healthy family systems have balanced levels of cohesion and flexibility. However, balance shouldn't be viewed as moderation. As Olson notes:

> Individuals and family systems need to balance their separateness versus togetherness on cohesion, and their level of stability versus change on flexibility. . . [Balanced] families do not always operate in a "moderate" manner. Being balanced means that a family system can experience extremes on the dimensions when appropriate, as in times of trauma or stress, but they do not typically operate at these extremes for long.
>
> (pp. 202–203)

In other words, balanced families are dynamic. They can respond to stress, change their levels of cohesion and flexibility based upon the context they are in or depending on the developmental life stage. At times these families may appear enmeshed or disengaged, chaotic or rigid, but these are adaptations that maintain the family's autonomy.

To test this model, Olson and his colleagues have developed Family Adaptability and Cohesion Evaluation Scale (FACES) and the Clinical Rating Scale. The FACES is a 62-item self-reported instrument that includes scales that assess cohesion, flexibility, and communication. The Clinical Rating Scale is an observation instrument. Raters observe families interacting and rate the families on cohesion, flexibility, and communication. Ratings are done on a bipolar scale ranging from "disengaged to enmeshed" on the cohesion scale, "rigid to chaotic" on the flexibility scale, and from "low to high" on the communication scale.

The ratings derived from these assessments can be plotted onto the Circumplex Model map. This map allows families and researchers to better understand how the dimensions of cohesion and flexibility work together to create balanced, mid-ranged, and unbalanced families. In addition, this map can be used to show developmental changes to the family. When a couple first starts to date, they may have high levels of cohesion and a balanced level of flexibility. But when the couple has a child, they may have to adapt to this new structure, by becoming more flexible to respond to the child's needs. At the same time their cohesion might be reduced as they turn their attention to raising an infant.

Many studies have used the FACES and the Clinical Rating Scale to evaluate the Circumplex Model. These studies have found that families that have balance function better than families that are unbalanced (Kouneski, 2000). Similar findings have been found for couples (Olson, Oslon-Sigg, & Larson, 2008). However, some research has found conflicting evidence for some of the hypotheses of the Circumplex Model.

For example, Volker Thomas and Timothy Ozechowski (2000) set out to test whether cohesion and flexibility predicted levels of family satisfaction and if cohesion and flexibility were distinct constructs that independently predicted family satisfaction levels, and if communication facilitated the expression of cohesion and flexibility in families. They recruited 70 couples, had them complete self-report scales, and then had them complete interactional tasks that lasted 30 minutes. These tasks were recorded and coded independently by two observers using the CRS. To their surprise, they found that cohesion and flexibility were not independent – they were highly correlated with each other. In addition, cohesion but not flexibility predicted family satisfaction – though the two constructs were correlated cohesion was the only one associated with family satisfaction. These results lend some support for the Circumplex Model, but challenge others. Specifically, it may be that capturing flexibility, even in observational research is difficult. It may be that flexibility occurs across time in response to stress or developmental changes and trying to measure it at one time point is insufficient.

This idea was tested by Stefanos Mastrotheodoros and his colleagues (2019). They examined how family functioning measured by the FACES-IV was longitudinally associated with depression, anxiety, and anger. They had 480 teenagers complete the FACES-IV, and depression, anxiety, and anger measured three times over a 12-month period. They found some interesting associations between these variables. Family functioning didn't predict worse symptoms over time; the opposite was found. Teenagers who "develop more symptoms of depression are statistically in higher risk of experiencing decreases in family functioning the following months compared to their peers who did not experience increases in depressive symptoms" (p. 8). These findings were contrary to what the authors predicted.

These results may be hinting at some of the same things Thomas and Ozechowski found. If the family is going to remain autonomous, it must adapt to the pressures within the system. If there is a member of the family with high levels of depression or anxiety, it may be that the family must reorganize some of the processes that they relied on previously. However, this reorganization is likely to happen across time. Processes that have been put in place to help the family maintain autonomy will likely take time to change. As the family adapts to the new stress, it may organize itself in a way that contains yet maintains the problematic symptoms – finding that has been supported by research. There are unique family profiles that are associated with unique psychological symptoms (Cerniglia et al., 2017).

Olson has argued something similar, suggesting that:

> The Circumplex Model is dynamic in that it assumes that changes can and do occur in the couple and family types over time. Families can move in any direction that the situation, stage of the family life cycle, or socialization of family members require . . . The changes can occur gradually over months or more rapidly. . . . These changes often occur without specific planning. Olson is highlighting the autonomous and adaptable nature of family systems. The family has processes, like cohesion, that link it together and create autonomy. In addition, families respond to the internal and external environment by adapting the autonomy-making processes to the current situation. The clinical symptoms present may be a cause or consequence of shifts in the family system's cohesion and flexibility.
>
> (p. 203)

The Family, Individual, and Genetic Systems

The systems that we have discussed this far – genes, individual, attachment, triangulation, and family – are all autonomous systems. Each has distinct processes that are more or less stable over time, have rules, and consume energy. Yet, each of these systems also interacts with each other and mutually influences each other. Genes affect our emotional responses, which affect the attachment and triangulation systems, which affect the cohesion and flexibility of the family system. The reverse order is also true. In fact, there are multiple ways in which each system is connected to, adapts to the other systems. It is often hard to tell where one system begins, and one system ends.

Research has begun to tease out how these systems influence each other. In 2020, Yayouk Willems and her colleagues examined the interactions of the genetic, individual, and family systems. Using a sample of more than 9,000 teenage twins, they explored how the family environment and genetic factors affected adolescents' ability to be self-regulated. They wanted to know if the family environment led to poorer adolescent self-control; if poor adolescent self-control resulted in more conflict; or if genes drive poor self-control. What they found speaks of the connectedness of the genetic, individual, and family systems:

> Family conflict predicts lower self-control in adolescence, with genetic factors also playing a role in explaining the association. . . . Families are at risk because they share the same genes, with the same

gene influencing the presence of family conflict and the risk of having low self-control. . . . Both of the underlying pathways explaining the association between family conflict and self-control – the contextual risk of family conflict and the genetic similarity within the family – manifest at the family level.

(pp. 6–7)

The family system affects adolescent self-control. Genes affect adolescent self-control. But they also interact and influence each other. The interaction between the genes and the family system affects adolescents' ability to express self-control. And because families share genes, it may be that families with genes that are more prone to poor self-control may result in greater levels of conflict at the family level.

Chapter Recap

The attachment and triangulation systems are the core relational systems that create the family system. The attachment system has been studied by researchers for decades. Whether through the Strange Situation experiment, the Still-Face experiment, or other means, today we have a clear understanding of the basic steps of an attachment relationship – we reach and invite connection; if we do not get the connection we seek, we protest or push for more connection; if that does not work, we then begin to turn away and shut down; then if we still are not connected, we go into meltdown. The goal of these steps is to help us reconnect so the person that we are in an attachment relationship with can help us regulate our distress. Attachment systems can include many dyads, but the most studied are between parents and child and between couples.

Attachment systems that are responsive, safe, and predictable can maintain their autonomy – generate connections, be sustained across time and during stress. But these attachment systems can also adapt to the current environment – create a safe space during stress, and allow people to explore when things are calm. When attachment systems are non-responsive and unsafe, this can lead to a breakdown of the system. The attachment system is the basic relational system. Humans are embedded in attachment systems from birth to death.

Overlapping attachment systems create the triangulation system. Since humans can and do have multiple attachment relationships, these systems tend to interact and create triangulation systems. The triangulation system develops because a significant relationship between two people in a family can have a powerful influence on a third family member, and vice versa, in mutually reinforcing ways. Triangles are created to stabilize or to reinforce attachment systems. Triangles can take on any number of constellations, but the most studied triangles are the parent–child triangle and the infidelity triangle.

Like the other systems of the family system, the triangulation system is autonomous and adaptable. The triangulation system has processes that serve to generate and maintain the family system – the interaction between three or more people may bind the system together. The formation of a triangle can also be an adaptation – it forms when the system experiences stress from inside or outside of the family system.

The attachment and triangulation systems and the process within are what structure the family system. If the attachment systems in a family are responsive and safe, and if the triangulation systems promote connection and individuality, then the family system will have processes that promote autonomy yet allow the system to adapt. These family systems tend to be cohesive and flexible. If the attachment systems of a family are unresponsive and unpredictable, and if the triangulation systems are used to alienate a family member or avoid conflict, these family systems may lack connection or may not be flexible.

Questions to Consider

1. Are there other relational systems that you think might help generate and maintain the family system? That help it adapt? If so, what are they? What are ways that researchers could study them?
2. What are other ways that the attachment system and triangulation system might interact or affect one another? Are one of these systems more influential than another on the family system? Why or why not?
3. Research has shown that attachment systems can look very different from each other. What factors might influence this? How might triangles play a role in this?
4. Olson's Circumplex Model provides a framework for understanding family system interactions. Are there things missing from this model? Is there a better way to describe family system interactions?

Chapter 4

The Sociocultural System

This is often the place where discussions of the family systems theory end. Having talked about the systems that exist within the family system, patterns of attachment and triangulation that create family dynamics, family systems theory discussions often say little about the broader environment that shapes the family system. Though much work has gone into discussing how social, cultural, and political forces should inform family therapy *models* (e.g., Falicov, 2012, 2014; McDowell, Knudson-Martin, & Bermudez, 2017); fewer have discussed how these forces are integral to family systems *theory*. For most of its history, family systems theory hasn't gone much beyond the border of the family.

In his outline of family systems theory, Alan Carr (2016) discussed how patterns in the family system may replicate in wider social systems.

> For example . . . a family-based pattern involving a strong mother-child coalition and a peripheral father may be replicated in the wider system with a strong coalition between the school counselor and the family and a peripheral relationship with the class teacher.
>
> (p. 25)

Carr is showing how processes in the family can be replicated in the wider social system, but his discussion is focused on how the family replicates its patterns outside of the family, not the effect of the broader social system on the family. Similarly, in Bowen's family systems theory, the focus is on the multigenerational system. Bowen has discussed at length regarding how intergenerational patterns affect current functioning. These patterns can create the culture in which the family is embedded, affecting how they respond and adapt to pressure. But Bowen spent little time detailing how larger social structures shape family's interactions, or how the social context of the family could affect differentiation of self.

If family systems theory is rooted in the idea of the family being an autonomous and adaptable system, then we cannot separate the family system from the broader system in which the family system is embedded.

As argued by Moreno and Mossio, "Autonomy is not independence. Biological organisms, as dissipative systems, can exist insofar as they maintain specific interactions with their surroundings" (p. 198). Bernd Rosslenbroich makes a similar argument:

> [N]o organisms can completely emancipate itself from the environment and thus always needs some environmental contract and exchange . . . The environment has its own structural dynamics, and although independent of the organism, it does not prescribe the changes in it. It induces a reaction in the organism, but the accepted changes are determined by the internal structures of the organism. It is the structure of the living system and its previous history of perturbations that determine what reactions the new perturbations will induce.
>
> (p. 228)

The family system is no different. The family system only exists because of the interactions it has with its environment. The environment that the family system is embedded has its own structural dynamics. These dynamics shape the autonomy processes of the family system.

The environment that the family system is embedded in is the sociocultural system. Teresa McDowell, Carmen Knudson-Martin, and Maria Bermudez defined the sociocultural system as:

> The interconnections of societal systems, culture, and power. This includes not only shared meanings that define culture, but dynamic interplay between societal systems that privilege some over others, resulting in uneven influence and opportunities based on social class, gender, race, ethnicity, language, sexual orientation, age, nation of origin, abilities, and looks.
>
> (p. 5)

Extensive research has shown how the sociocultural system impacts the family and can result in changes to the autonomy and adaptive processes. Our discussion here will focus on the factors that span generations and cultures: power, privilege, oppression.

Power, Privilege, and Oppression in the Sociocultural System

Power is a systemic concept. Those with power can decide who has access to resources and how those resources are used. Those with power can also have a direct influence on others and on their behaviors. Power is what gives people access to privilege. Privilege is unearned access to resources based on membership of an advantaged group. Depending on the culture, time, and location in which a family resides, they may have more or less privileges based on their identities. Often those with power and privilege use it to oppress other. Oppression is a creation of social and structural processes that are used to diminish or immobilize groups of people.

In 2004, Iris Young expanded upon this definition of oppression by describing what she calls "five faces of oppression." She argues that the five faces of oppression are comprehensive and useful categories, but that they are not necessarily isolated. People can and do experience multiple forms of oppression. Further she argues that:

> Oppression has often been perpetuated by a conceptualization of group difference in terms of unalterable essential natures that determines what group members deserve or are capable of, and that exclude groups so entirely from one another that they have no similarities or overlapping attributes.
>
> (p. 44)

This falsehood allows those in power to justify their use of the five faces of oppression to maintain their privileges and access to resources.

The first face of oppression is exploitation.

> The central insight expressed in the concept of exploitation . . . is that this oppression occurs through a steady process of the transfer of the results of . . . one social group to benefit another. . . . Exploitation enacts a structural relation between social groups. Social rules about what work is, who does what for whom, how work is compensated, and the social process by which the results of work are appropriated operate to enact relations of power and inequality.
>
> (p. 46)

Those in power will often create false narratives around what work should be valued and what shouldn't be. Then they use this narrative to maintain the social systems that exploit people whose work or social category they deem worthy of exploitation. This results in few being able to amass an abundance of resources at the expense of others.

The second face of oppression is marginalization. Marginalization consists of the social and structural processes that serve to push groups of people from useful patriation in society. At its most extreme edge, marginalization can result in total material deprivation and/or extermination. Young argues:

> Marginalization is perhaps the most dangerous form of oppression . . . Because they depend on bureaucratic institutions for support or services,

> the old, the poor, and the mentally or physically disabled are subject to patronizing, punitive, demeaning, and arbitrary treatment by polices and people associated with welfare bureaucracies. Being dependent in our society implies being legitimately subject to the often arbitrary and invasive authority of social service providers and other public and private administrators, who enforce rules with which the marginal must comply, and otherwise exercise power over the conditions of their lives. (p. 50)

The process of marginalization, in many cases, creates a permanent class of individuals who are confined to the margins of society, without access to or power to have real participation in their societies.

Powerlessness is the third face of oppression. Young sees this face of oppression in the professional class. Professionals "have some authority over others . . . Nonprofessionals, on the other hand, lack autonomy, and in both their working and consumer-client lives often stand under the authority of professions" (p. 53). This difference results in the professionals and nonprofessionals having different cultures, neighborhoods, and a different level of respectability. "In restaurants, banks, hotels, real estate offices, and many other such public places, as well as in the media, professionals typically receive more respectful treatment than nonprofessionals" (p. 53). This lack of respect further reinforces and exacerbates aspects to resources and participation in social life.

The fourth face of oppression is cultural imperialism. "Cultural imperialism involves the paradox of experiencing oneself as invisible at the same time that one is marked out as different" (p. 56). Through cultural imperialism, those in power get to universalize their experience and normalize their culture, placing value upon those things that they see as valued. They also get to determine the narrative around events and elements that occur in the society. Those who are culturally imperialized are often "stamped with an essence." They become the dominate narrative of groups that are rendered inescapable.

> Just as everyone knows that the earth goes around the sun, so everyone knows that gay people are promiscuous, that Indians are alcoholics, and that women are good with children. White males, on the other hand, insofar as they escape group marking, can be individuals. (p. 55)

The central injustice of cultural imperialism is that the oppressed group's experiences and interpretations are disregarded in favor of the culture that is imposed on the oppressed group.

Violence is the final face of oppression. Violence is common throughout history as a means of gaining or maintaining power and privilege.

Young argues that violence is both social and systemic. "It is social given that everyone knows it happens and will happen again. It is always at the horizon of the social imagination" (p. 57). Violence is also systemic "because it is directed at members of a group simply because they are members of that group" (p. 57). In countries across the world, women have reasons to fear rape, and gays and lesbians live under constant threat of violence. Those in power often justify their use of violence through the cultural imperialism. Because the dominate culture has stamped certain groups with certain attributes, it uses these attributes that it has assigned to the group to justify violence against them.

Two examples demonstrate how the faces of oppression have created our modern sociocultural system. The first example is the creation of race. In his book *How to Be an Antiracist*, Ibram X. Kendi chronicles the creation of modern-day racial groups, and how it was done to help some amass and keep power and privilege. Kendi points to Prince Henry the Navigator as the "first character in the history of racist power (p. 39)". In the fifteenth century, Prince Henry sponsored voyages to West Africa to enslave exclusively Africans. Slave trading existed before Prince Henry, but previous enslavers were enslaving what today would be considered Europeans, Arabs, and Africans. To excuse this practice, King Alfonso V of Portugal commissioned a royal chronicler and commander of Prince Henry's army to write an effusive biography of Henry. The biographer, Gomes de Zurara, was the "first race maker and crafter or racist ideas (p. 39).

De Zurara documented Henry's first major slave action, writing that some of "the captives were 'white enough to look upon, and well proportion' while others were 'like mulattoes' or 'as black as Ethiops, and so ugly'" (p. 40). Despite the variety of skin tones, size, and appearance, de Zurara combined all of them into one single group. Kendi notes:

> Gomes de Zurara grouped all those people from Africa into a single race for that very reason: to create hierarchy, the first racist idea . . . Prince Henry's racist policy of slave trading came first . . . After nearly two decades of slave trading, King Alfonso asked Gomes de Zurara to defend the lucrative commerce in human lives, which he did through the construction of a Black race, an invented group upon which he hung racist ideas. This cause and effect – a racist power creates racist policies out of raw self-interest; the racist policies necessitate racist ideas to justify them – lingers over the life of racism.
>
> (pp. 40, 42)

These same processes were replicated when colonizers came to the new world. The colonizers wanted to be able to justify taking resources, killing and enslaving indigenous people. They created racial hierarchies to justify the self-serving policies.

These processes are still evident today. The echoes of race making allow certain groups to retain power and privilege, while systematically disenfranchising and marginalizing others. Again, as Kendi notes:

> Latinx and Asian and African and European and Indigenous and Middle Eastern: These six races – at least in the American context – are fundamentally power identities, because race is fundamentally a power construct of blended difference that live socially. Race creates new forms of power: the power to categorize and judge, elevate and downgrade, include and exclude. Race makers use that power to process distinct individuals, ethnicities, and nationalities into monolithic races.
>
> (p. 38)

The race-making processes demonstrate the use of the five faces of oppression to amass and maintain power and access to resources. In his recounting of race making, Kendi is showing how exploitation, marginalization, culture imperialism, and violence worked together to create new forms and structures of power and to justify the actions that allow those in power to stay in power. The creation of race and its consequences are still present in today's culture.

The second example is marriage. Though it is frequently romanticized, many have argued that marriage is an institution that has served to keep power and privilege in the hands of certain groups. In her 2017 book, *Against Marriage*, Clare Chambers argues that historically and currently the process of marriage has disadvantaged women as well as gender and sexual minorities. Chambers lays out her case against marriage saying,

> Marriage . . . as an institution [is] founded on patriarchy and heteronormativity . . . its reform to include same-sex couple does not do enough to make it egalitarian since they very idea of marriage remains rooted in forms of intimacy that are associated with heterosexual and male privilege, and that even a radically informed marriage or civil union inevitably brings about inequality between those who are partnered and those who are not.
>
> (p. 46)

Further she suggests:

> Marriage is fundamentally a gendered institution. It has been the main mechanism for maintaining the gendered division of labour, for

regulating men's access to women's bodies, and for giving men ownership and control of children. Marriage provides a structure within which men and women are represented as opposites: complementary but stratified, roles separate and ranked. He works, she cooks and cleans; his work is paid, her is not; his work is borne of power and entitlement, her of love and duty. The state recognition of marriage has been the state recognition of this gendered arrangement.

(p. 201)

Chambers isn't saying that people can't have satisfying, happy marriages that promote well-being and health. Research has shown time and time again that marriage can benefit physical and emotional well-being (Carr & Springer, 2010). She is arguing for the end of state-recognized marriage.

She is suggesting that by sanctioning and promoting marriage, governments are maintaining an institution that historically and presently consists of the five faces of oppression. In different-sex marriages, women's work is not valued. Women still do most of the household labor and are often exclusively responsibly for the emotional labor – for neither of which they receive monetary compensation. Governments have used the institution of marriage to create cultural imperialism to stratify groups based on who could marry and who could not. In many countries, marriage has been used to marginalize religious, racial, and sexual minorities. Governments have also sanctioned marriage-based violence. Rape in marriage affects millions each year, and in many countries, it is still legal. In the United states, marital rape wasn't fully criminalized until 1993 (Yllö & Torres, 2016).

Chambers argues for what she calls a "marriage-free state."

> The marriage-free state starts by identifying the right and duties that are appropriate for the unmarried. It then applies those rights and duties to everyone . . . At its most basic the marriage-free state simply demands that the rights and duties that apply to the unmarried should apply to everyone.
>
> (p. 202)

In a marriage-free state, people could still get married, if they choose, but these marriages wouldn't come with specific privileges nor expectations.

> The marriage-free state does not rule out weddings, ceremonies, or celebrations. It does not rule out stability, or family, or commitment, or devotion. It does not rule out love. It *does* rule out the idea that those values are the preserve of one very particular relationship format. It does rule out the state proceeding in such a way

as to disadvantage, discriminate against, or stigmatize those whose families are not structured according to this format. It aims to secure equality for all, regardless of relationship or family type.

(p. 204)

Chambers is arguing that the privileges afforded to those who are married should be afforded to all. More and more, marriage is becoming an institution for those with privilege to maintain their privilege. Governments across the globe provide incentives for people to get and stay married; they determine who can and can't get married; and culture looks down on those, especially women, who choose not to marry. This inequity, Chambers argues, could be rectified if privileges were afforded to all, not just those who are married.

The Consequences of Power, Privilege, and Oppression

Research has shown the effects that power, privilege, oppression, and the creation of inequitable social structures have on families. One such area is income inequality. Across the globe, the effect of marriage and other inequitable institutions and policies can be seen on the pay for men and women – men get paid substantially more than women for the same work. In South Korea, men earn on average 33.59% more than women; in France it's 15.5%. The difference becomes even more apparent, when we examine the intersection of gender and race. In 2015 in the United States, the median hourly earnings for a white man was $21, black men made $15, and Hispanic men made $14. White women had median hourly earnings of $17, while black women made $13, and Hispanic women made $12 (Patten, 2016).

More and more, the inequitable, racist, and sexist structures that exist have resulted in fewer and fewer having more power, more resources, and more privileges. In the United States, from 1979 to 2007 the average income of the top 1% of families quadrupled. The trend has continued. In 2016, the top 1% of families in the United Stated controlled 39% of the total wealth in the United States (Stone, Trisi, Sherman, & Debot, 2015). This inequity hasn't just occurred in the United States but has happened across the globe.

In 2018, The World Economic Forum pulled together data from multiple sources to get a glimpse of income inequality across multiple countries. In those considered "advanced economies" (e.g., Germany, Italy, Japan, and the United Kingdom), income inequality increased or remained the same in 20 of the 29 countries. In the countries considered "emerging economies" (e.g., Argentina, China, Mexico, and Nigeria), income inequality improved but was still at extreme levels.

Research suggests that when those at the top have more wealth, the whole country suffers. In 2015, Era Dabla-Norris and her colleagues set out to understand global income inequality and how it affects economic growth. In their analysis of data from across multiple countries, they found that:

> [I]f the income share of the top 20 percent (the rich) increase, then GDP growth actually declines over the medium term, suggesting that benefits do not trickle down. In contrast, an increase in the income share of the bottom 20 percent (the poor) is associated with higher GDP growth.
>
> (p. 4)

In other words, when those with power and privilege hold on to their resources, this slows down overall economic growth.

Without access to resources, families are limited in how they can respond, which can result in stress, conflict, and other problems. When families experience job insecurity this shapes how they interact and respond in their relationships. Working-class men, who can experience job insecurity, report using more domineering masculine behaviors because they felt they couldn't provide for their families. This occurred even when their partners resented these behaviors (Sassler & Miller, 2017). Those with job and income insecurity often see their relationships like they see their jobs – something that can be taken away without warning. Those who haven't experienced job insecurity often use language to describe their relationships that suggests their relationships can endure stress and still stay intact. Those who have experienced job insecurity often use language that suggests a brittleness to their relationships (Pugh, 2015).

This brittleness may result from the toll that lack of access to resources takes on relationships. In 2008, Matthew Desmond began an ethnographic study of the effect that income, job, and housing insecurity can have on families. From May to September 2008, he rented a trailer in a very poor, predominantly white, trailer park in Milwaukee. Right after that, he moved into a rooming house in an impoverished predominantly black neighborhood in Milwaukee for the same number of months. During this time, he spent on average five days a week observing and participating in the everyday lives of his neighbors. He would carry a digital recorder and a notepad to capture things he observed and the nuances of interactions.

Throughout this process he found that:

> A lack of resources in addition to structural and legal barriers prevent poor kin from helping; middle-class kin also withheld support from their less fortunate relatives, justifying their actions by citing past aid understood to be more than sufficient or by affixing to their kin

a collection of base quality that rendered them underserving. Often, then, rather than turning to their kin, evicted tenants reach out to strangers ... Through a kind of accelerated and simulated intimacy, virtual strangers quickly became "best friends" or "sisters." ... But almost inexorably, disposable ties would snap under the weight of any number of factors, including the tendency to from multiple ties with individuals who would then compete with one another. When disposable ties were disposed of, individuals began looking for a new relationship or might attempt to approach a relative. This looping pattern of forming, using, and burning ties, this weary rhythm – make a friend, use a friend, lose a friend – best captures an essential survival strategy tenant regularly employed.

(pp. 1321–1322)

These social bonds, though temporary and fragile, are born out of necessity. Because access to income, housing, and other resources is insecure for many, often their family and other close relationships are labeled inferior or problematic. When in fact, these individuals, families, and the ties they are creating are adaptations to respond to an inequitable environment. With access to resources that others enjoy and have in abundance, their family relationships would likely look what we would deem "healthy."

Income inequality is not the only reason where power structures affect families, but it is also evident in health outcomes. According to the World Health Organization (WHO), there is a 36-year life expectancy gap between countries. A child born in Japan is expected to live 36 years longer than a child born in Malawi. In Europe, the underage child mortality rate is 13 out of 1000; in Chad, one out of every five children die before the age of five. Women in the richest 20% of the global population are up to 20 times more likely to have their birth attended by a trained health-care provider than women who are poor. The WHO estimates that if this gap is closed, the lives of more than 700,000 women could be saved over four years.

The University of Oslo – Global Commission on Global Governance for Health (Ottersen et al., 2014) argues that the root of these and the many other health inequities are power, privilege, and oppression.

The root causes of health inequity lie in the unequal distribution of power, money, and resources. Power disparities and dynamics suffuse all aspects of life: relations between men and women, or old and young people, as well as between countries, firms and organizations. Upheld by contemporary societal and global norms and policies, which are in turn maintained by those actors with the most power, power asymmetries persist.

(p. 634)

The racist, sexist, and other oppressive structures that are present throughout the world result in vastly different outcomes for families. If you are lucky enough to be born in a country that has more power or privilege, or into a group within a country that has more access to privilege, you are likely to lead a healthier life.

You can also see the effect of power structures within countries. The United States has been labeled the "world leader in health inequity" by the Washington Post. In the United states, many of the largest chronic health conditions all vary by racial/ethnic group. But let us just examine one area of health inequity in the United States – heart disease.

Heart disease is the leading cause of death in the United States (CDCP, 2019). It is responsible for about 600,000 deaths each year. Though it is still a major health issue, the treatment and prevention of heart disease has increased dramatically. Because of that, deaths associated with heart disease have been going down since the 1980s. However, your risk of death from heart disease varies by race.

In a study using data of 50 of the largest US cities, Maureen R. Benjamins and her colleagues examined deaths associated with heart disease between 1990 and 1994 and between 2005 and 2009. Across the United States, they found that blacks were 30% more likely to die of heart disease than whites. In some cities this rate was much larger – in Washington, DC blacks were 90% more likely to die of heart disease than whites. "White disparity in heart disease mortality translates into an astounding 19,448 excess Black deaths per year or an average of 53 excess Black deaths per day" (p. 973). They also found that though deaths associated with heart disease are down, the difference between whites and blacks grew between 1990 and 2009.

Racist ideas used to prop up racist policies have real-world consequences. In their 2017 paper, Zinzi D. Bailey and her colleagues traced the connection of racist policies and ideas to health inequities, concluding that:

> Since the American colonial period, public and private institutions have reinforced each other, maintaining racial hierarchies that have allowed white Americans, across generations, to earn more and consolidate more wealth than non-white Americans, and maintain political dominance. This structural racism has had substantial role in shaping the distribution of social determinants of health and the population health profile of the USA, including persistent health inequities.
>
> (p. 1461)

The difference in outcomes in heart disease for black and white Americans is a direct result of the racist policies that existed and continue to exist. To create equity, policies that reinforce power hierarchies must be changed.

Autonomy and Adaptation in the Sociocultural System

Power, privilege, oppression and the policies and structure they create are the environment within which the family system is embedded. Whether we are aware of it or not, these forces are working together to shape families. Though these forces do not prescribe the way a family adapts to stress or maintain autonomy, all families must interact with the sociocultural system.

In their 2018 article, Sharde McNeil Smith and Antoinette M. Landor proposed the Sociocultural Family Stress model to understand autonomy and adaptive processes that occur between the family and the sociocultural system. This model was primarily developed to describe family processes in African American families, but the concepts are useful for many families.

Smith and Landor propose that the family's social position influences their ability to adapt to stress. This social position may determine the resources and coping strategies they have available to deal with stress, their perception of the stressor, and the amount of stress and reliance they had before the new stressor occurred. They also point out that the structure of the family may also influence their response to stress. The dominant narrative in the United States is that families must include married partners, as such single parent households may experience more stress since they "deviate" from the culturally determined norms. "Socially and culturally diverse families, or those who are different from White, heteronormative, two-parent families are deemed categorically different in our society and consequently are conferred disadvantaged social status" (p. 483). In addition, their model proposes that families are also embedded in a sociocultural system that is racist, classist, sexist, and heteronormative. The social position, family structure, and the racist, classist, sexist, and heteronormative polices and structures combine to affect the family's ability to adapt to stress.

For example, if a family member has a heart attack, the family's response to this stress is dependent on many factors in the sociocultural system. First, depending on whether or not they have health insurance, they may have to think about other ways to get the person to the hospital – as noted Christine DiGangi in *USA Today* in 2017, sometimes a two-mile ambulance ride can cost $2,700. Once they get to the hospital, the sociocultural system has an effect on the care they receive. If the family member is a women, she may receive suboptimal care for her heart condition (Molix, 2014), and, if she is in lingering pain afterwards, she may also not get adequate care (Chen et al., 2008).

After the family member is discharged from the hospital, the sociocultural system may exacerbate or reduce the stress in the family. If the person who had the heart attack was contributing to the family income, the loss of that income may result in food insecurity and or rely on safety net systems in place in their community. Or they may reach out to friends and family members to provide financial support during recovery. The person who is caring for the family member may also be increasing their risk of health problems in the future. More than 50% of women in the United States will care for a family member at some point in their lives. Women who take on caregiving responsibility for family members following a heart attack are typically 50 years old and older and are often unemployed (Aggarwal & Mosca, 2009). Providing care puts these women at risk for depression, social isolation, and weight gain – all risk factors for cardiovascular disease. In other words, by providing care for a family member who has had a heart attack, women are increasing their own risk of having a heart attack (Aggarwal & Mosca, 2009).

Often, the adaptation strategies of families that live in oppressive sociocultural systems are viewed as dysfunctional or problematic. The way these families adapt is often used to reinforce messages about their social group. Instead of recognizing the injustice, oppression and inequity in the sociocultural system, these families may be labeled lazy, lacking "family values" or incapable of solving their problems or pulling themselves up from their bootstraps. Yet, when you examine the sociocultural system in which the family is embedded, the adaptations that this family is making are often a reflection of that system and not the family. These adaptations aren't indicative of problematic families but of the problematic environment in which they are embedded.

The sociocultural system is the context in which all the other research summarized in previous chapters are embedded. The genetic, individual, attachment, triangulation, and family systems are all blanketed in the sociocultural system. The autonomy-making and adaptive processes in each of those systems can't be understood without understanding the sociocultural system. Often, research may label families "healthy" or "unhealthy," attachment processes "secure" or "insecure," or emotional reactions "good" or "bad." But these labels often fail to consider the sociocultural system. The family system can't be separated from the sociocultural system.

Chapter Recap

No system is independent of its environment. Though the environment doesn't force a system to act or adapt in a specific way, it does impact it. The family system is embedded in the sociocultural system. This system – defined as the interconnections of societal system, culture, and power – blankets all aspects of the family system. Though the sociocultural system has many components, power, privilege, and oppression are core to this system. Those with power and privilege often use them to oppress other. Oppression has many faces including exploitation, marginalization, powerlessness, cultural imperialism, and violence.

These faces of oppression helped create our modern sociocultural system. The faces of oppression resulted in the creation of race – a category used by those with power to amass power, privilege, and resources, and marriage – a socially sanctioned institution that has historically worked to oppress and remove rights from specific groups. The racist, sexist, and other oppressive structures that are present throughout the world result in vastly different outcomes for families – resulting in few having sufficient resources and many struggling to survive. The social position, family structure, and the racist, classist, sexist, and heteronormative polices and structures that exist in a family's environment all work together to affect the family's ability to adapt to stress and by extension maintain their autonomy. Much research has documented how the sociocultural system serves to oppress and undermine families that don't hold privilege status and then blame them for not being able to adapt successfully to insurmountable barriers, stress, and lack of resources.

Questions to Consider

1. What other important factors go into the creation of the sociocultural system? How do these factors impact families?
2. In this chapter, I argued that family systems theory often fails to go beyond the border of the family. Would you agree with this argument? What evidence supports your assertions?
3. Clare Chambers makes a case for a marriage-free state. Do you agree or disagree with this position? What is the rationale for the position you take?
4. What is your reaction to the research on income inequality and health inequities? How might family therapist serve to improve or worsen these outcomes?
5. In this chapter, the work of Ibram X. Kendi is summarized. He recounts the development of race categories and how this has led to injustices and inequities. How do family therapists perpetuate racism? What are ways in which family therapists could become anti-racist?

Part 2

Linking the Evidence to Theory

We've now examined evidence of each of the systems that create the family system. But does this evidence support the idea that the family is an autonomous system and an adaptable system? To answer this question, we need to be clear about what we mean by autonomy and what we mean by adaptation. Without a clear definition and understanding of these terms, we can't have a clear understanding of whether the evidence supports the idea of the family being autonomous and adaptable.

What's more, we need to understand the limitations of family systems theory and the evidence that supports it. As discussed in Chapter 1, research and theory have a reciprocal relationship. As we get more research, we sometimes must change our theory; as we change our theory, it leads us to better hypotheses. By understanding the limitations and gaps in the research supporting the claims I've made here, we may be able to develop ways to conduct research that can fill in these gaps. This research may support the hypotheses of family systems theory proposed here; or it may undermine them. If the latter is the case, these would need to be amended or discarded based on the new evidence.

In this section, we will spend time defining both autonomy and adaptation. We will see, based on the definitions we are using, if the evidence is sufficient to support the hypothesis that the family is an autonomous and adaptable system. In addition, we'll spend time talking about the assumptions, limitations, and caveats that accompany family systems theory and its hypotheses as well as discuss ways that these issues can be addressed.

Chapter 5

The Family as an Autonomous System

Does the evidence support the hypothesis that the family is an autonomous system?

Before we answer this question, we need to be clear about what biological autonomy is and what it is not. We discussed this a bit in Chapter 1, but I think we need to revisit it again. In its typical usage, autonomy is associated with the idea of independence. It is the ability to act in accordance with what a person wants or thinks is right. When defining autonomy, we think about pursuing our own goals, following our own directives, and having agency over what we do. This is an important type of autonomy, but this isn't the kind of autonomy we are talking about here.

The idea of autonomy is also present in family therapy models and research. In his 2020 paper, *Inviting Autonomy Back to the Table*, Jared Anderson proposes that autonomy in family therapy models is different from how autonomy is typically defined. He argues that when family therapists discuss autonomy, they often mischaracterize it. He writes:

> The misinformed caricature is that autonomy in intimate partnerships is equal to individuation (i.e., separateness), lack of connection, and emotional separation. In other words, the more autonomous you are, the less connected you are and vice versa. This caricature is both unfortunate and wrong, but it continues to be advanced.... Individuality (autonomy) does not stand in *separation from* or *opposition to* others. It is not the isolation and separateness of rugged individualism, or the notion that *in order to be me, I have to distance myself from you*. Nor is it synonymous with traditional romantic notions of independence (nonreliance) or freedom (lack of constraints) which are often antirelational ... Autonomy is self-determination, assenting to or owning one's beliefs and values and the behavior that follows.
> (pp. 3–4)

Anderson further describes different types of autonomy, including trait autonomy (the individual level of autonomy that is relatively stable across time) and relationship autonomy (the degree to which your actions and motivations for being in a relationship are self-controlled versus externally controlled).

Though Anderson brings up many strong arguments, his discussion of autonomy is also different from the core ideas of biological autonomy expressed by other systems theorists and researchers. If we return to the definition of biological autonomy provided in Chapter 1, it has three core ideas:

1. Autonomous systems have processes that contribute to the generation and maintenance of their existence.
2. The processes are interdependent, differentiated, rule based, hierarchical, and create a boundary between the system and the environment.
3. The processes are relatively stable across time.

Autonomy, in the biological sense, is about the processes that create the system, not necessarily about the people in the system. As we'll see later in this chapter, I argue that Anderson's ideas are an important and an embedded part of family systems autonomy, but they aren't all of it. If the family system is a biologically autonomous system, then evidence should support each of the core ideas of biological autonomy.

Processes

I've been using another word that, before we go any further, I want to define, *process*. Systems theorists and researchers suggest that biological autonomy exists when a system has *processes* that generate and maintain the system. In each of the three components of biological autonomy, the word *process* is used. In the previous chapters, I've talked about the science related to systems that create the family system, but a process is different from a system. If you remember, von Bertalanffy defined a system as "a set of elements standing in inter-relations" (p. 55). For elements to be interrelated, he argued, the interactions of elements within a system must be different from the interactions of elements outside of the system.

Processes are what create interrelatedness. They are what links the elements together. If there are no processes that tie elements together, then there is no system. These links are what makes the interactions between the family systems elements different from the interactions outside of the system. But processes are only autonomy creating when they meet certain criteria. As noted earlier, they must be connected to other processes in the system (interdependence) and at the same time, must be distinguishable from the other processes (differentiated). They must have patterns, steps, or rules to follow (rule based) that are somewhat predictable, be hierarchical, and they must exist across time and therefore be at least somewhat resistant to change.

If the family is an autonomous system, there must be processes that link the diverse elements in the system – it must be present in and span the genetic, individual, attachment, triangulation, and sociocultural systems. Using these definitions and criteria, research points to three core processes that create the interrelatedness of the family system. There are more processes than the three discussed here, but I will focus on these because of the vast amounts of evidence there is to support them.

Threat-Response Processes

First are the threat-response processes (also referred to as stress-response processes). At the most basic level the threat-response processes are concerned with survival. The process of natural selection in the genetic system is a threat-response process that allows for survival across time. The epigenome in the genetic system also allows for information to be gathered in the environment and changes the genome with the goal of furthering the chances for survival presently and across generations.

In the individual system, the nervous system has evolved to help us fight, freeze, or flee when we encounter threats, and these are connected to the emotional systems of FEAR, PANIC/GRIEF and RAGE that are concerned with responding to threats. Emotion regulation allows us to upcycle or downcycle our emotions to respond to threats. The attachment system also has threat-response processes. We can't handle many threats on our own – but if we have an important other around to protect or fight with us, we are better able to respond to threats to our survival. Similarly, the triangulation system also has threat-response processes. If there is tension in an attachment system, bringing in a third person may help the attachment system survive, or it may create a new attachment system so the original one can be discarded. All of this works together to ensure survival.

In addition, the sociocultural system plays an important role in survival. Given the structures and policies of a given society, some will have more access to resources than others. Those with the fewest resources are more likely to have threats to their survival. If your society/culture has created structures and policies that marginalize and stigmatize certain groups, these groups will have threat-response processes that can be in constant operation, leading to stress in all systems.

The idea of the role of survival in family systems theory is not new. In his summary of family systems theory, Alan Carr (2016) also emphasized the importance of survival. His first hypothesis reads:

> The family is a social system which supports the survival of its members. . . . Other social systems, such as work groups or sports teams, may be established to fulfill functions such as manufacturing goods,

providing services, or competing in games. In contrast, the primary objective of a family system is supporting the survival of its members.

(p. 16)

But threats aren't just about survival. In the family system, other types of threats can activate these same threat-response processes. Family therapy theorists have emphasized two important factors that can activate threat-response processes. These factors have been called different names – Bowen called them "individuality and togetherness," Minuchin called them "sense of belonging and sense of being separate," or more recently, as noted earlier, Jared Anderson has referred to these ideas as "attachment and autonomy." But whatever language is used, these factors are major activators of threat-response process.

If a person feels like they don't belong to a group, or there is potential they might lose people with whom they are closely connected, it is likely that this will activate threat-response processes. This may be especially evident in the individual, attachment, and triangulation systems. Jaak Panksepp has argued that the PANIC/GRIEF emotional system focuses on this fear of losing connections with others. He has suggested that all mammals experience panic when they are separated from an attachment figure, which leads them to engage in behaviors that try to close the distance.

In humans, physical distance from an attachment figure isn't the only thing that can activate threat-response processes, so can the loss of intimacy. As noted in the attachment research on demand–withdraw patterns, if we feel that we are losing a connection with a partner, we might start to pursue more and more closeness. This could give rise to the four patterns that Sue Johnson has summarized (i.e., criticize/withdraw, attack–attack, freeze and flee, and chaos and ambivalence. Similarly, as demonstrated in the Still-Face experiment, when infants experience loss of connection with an attachment figure, they also engage in behaviors to reengage the person.

If, for whatever reason, we can't reengage attachment figures, threat-response processes can have us triangulate in another person. If a couple is fighting and partners can't reconnect, a partner may turn to their parents for comfort. This may allay the current fear of disconnection but reinforce a process that has the couple turn to another member of the family during times of stress, potentially stabilizing or undermining the couple's relationship. Threat-response processes, activated by belongingness, are central to the formation of triangulation systems.

The sociocultural system also plays an important role in the sense of belonging and togetherness. The structures that are created in a society to help those at the top retain power and privilege are often about dictating who belongs and who doesn't. In many countries, those in power determine who and who can't marry, fall in love, or have children. They may also determine those who are "good" – belonging to the privileged group, and those who are "bad" – belonging to the marginalized group, and what is the "correct" way to belong and what is "incorrect."

A sense of belonging, connectedness, or togetherness isn't the only factor that activates threat-response processes, so do threats to our self-determination, our individuality, or our sense of being separate. As Kerr and Bowen discussed in *Family Evaluation*, "individuality . . . refers to the capacity to be an individual *while being a part of the group*" (p. 63). The fear of being abandoned or not having a sense of belonging is juxtaposed with threats to our self-determination. If we want to pursue something and those closest to us don't want us to, or if we are feeling that being connected to someone threatens our sense of self, threat-response processes become active.

In the individual system we can see many threat-response processes. If our individuality is threatened, we may fight or flee. Or we may engage emotion regulation strategies that try to help stay connected to while maintaining our sense of being separate; we may avoid the emotions or suppress them. These responses give rise to activation of threat-responses in the attachment system. If we are sensing a threat to our individuality or self-determination, we may withdraw from attachment figures, or we may start an argument to create more space. In addition, we may try to create emotional space by triangulating a third person. We may form a coalition with another person to try and push the person we feel is too close away. This way we maintain our connection to a group, but we can still have a sense of self.

In the sociocultural system, the five faces of oppression are used to decide who has individuality and who does not. Oppression has been used to dehumanize certain groups of people or send them to the margins of society. In the United States, for example, slavery, Jim Crow, and other laws and policies institutionalized racist oppression in American society. When those who are oppressed have resisted, they are often met with violence – which is typically justified by denying groups of people a sense of humanity or individuality. When we make people a group rather than individuals, those in power feel justified in assigning characteristics to a group that they then use to rationalize their oppression and continue to limit their access to resources.

Belonging and Individuality Processes

Threat-response processes are activated when a sense of belonging or individuality is threatened because belonging and individuality are the other two processes that generate and maintain the family system. Together, these are the three core processes that maintain the family system. Just like the threat-response system, the belonging and individuality processes are present in each system that creates the family system, though in each system these processes are different.

Belonging processes are present in the genetic system. As Apicella and Silk (2019) argued, the process of natural selection may have given rise to humans' ability to cooperate. To ensure our survival, we evolved processes that make us want to feel connected and benefit from connecting. Part of this evolution resulted in the social engagement system. This system is perhaps one of the main drivers of belonging processes. As Stephen Porges (2018) argued the social engagement system is what allowed humans to co-opt some of the threat-response processes to engage in play and intimacy, to care for offspring, and to cooperate. In addition, the engagement of the emotional systems of CARE, LUST, and PLAY are all belonging processes.

The attachment and triangulation systems each have belonging processes. The connection between two people, whether that be to provide care and protection, to be emotionally or physically intimate, or to create safety and responsiveness are all belonging processes that are found in the attachment system. Because one person can't sustain each of these processes all the time, it is necessary for us to have others whom we can connect with. This gives rise to the belonging processes in the triangulation system. Having multiple people who we can connect with when one attachment figure is unable is a triangulation-belonging process that helps support and reinforce the attachment system. And as noted earlier, the sociocultural system also has belonging processes that are often dictated by those who have power and privilege.

Individuality processes also span the systems that create the family system. These processes are the "autonomy" that Jared Anderson (2020) described. In the individual system, the mirror neuron and the mentalizing systems have key individuality processes. These systems work as social detection and social evaluation systems. They allow us to recognize important cues in our environment and infer what others might be thinking, which allows us to respond based on ways in which we can understand and maintain our self in a social system. Similarly, the ability to regulate our emotions is an individuality process. By not only reacting to our emotional experiences but regulating them, we are able to create a sense of separateness between ourselves and those in our social systems. Through emotional regulation we can understand that the emotions of others, though we may sense them, doesn't dictate how we must respond.

The attachment system also has individuality processes. As Mikulincer and Shaver (2007) argued, "when attachment relationships function well, a person learns that distance and autonomy are completely compatible with closeness and reliance on others" (p. 13). In other words, the belongingness processes of the attachment system help create and maintain individuality processes. If we feel safe and connected, we have a greater ability to play, explore, and have a sense of separateness. The individuality processes in the triangulation system help reinforce and sustain the attachment system. Since our attachment figures can't meet all of our needs, when we have multiple people to turn to, we are better able to regulate our emotions and engage in play and explorations. As noted earlier, the sociocultural system also has individuality processes. Often the sociocultural system decides who is an individual and who is a group, and then uses the group designation, or the lack of individuality, to oppress others and keep power.

Just as the threat-response system can be activated when our sense of belonging or individuality is threatened, belonging and individuality processes can be activated when the family is under threat. If a person in the system were to lose a job, the family may amplify their belonging processes to provide support and care during stress. Or it may provide greater self-determination whereby the family allows the family member who lost the job to take the time to explore their next steps and empower them to make decisions. Or, it may do both.

The response of the belonging and individuality processes in the presence of threat is indicative of the balance hypotheses of Olson's Circumplex Model. Olson suggested that "Being a balanced family means that a family system can experience extreme of [belonging or individuality] when appropriate, as in times of trauma or stress, but they do not typically operate at these extremes for long" (p. 203). In other words, when a family experiences a threat to its survival, families will intensify processes that they think will help ensure their survival. The belonging and individuality processes can be activated at different levels and at different times to try to maintain the survival of the family.

Family System Processes and Autonomy Components

These three processes have shown that they meet one part of the components needed to be autonomous and sustaining and generation processes – they are interdependent. When our belongingness or individuality is threatened, the threat-response process is activated. When we sense threats to our family system, we activate our belonging and individuality process. Each of these processes works together to sustain the family system. These processes are interdependent in that they generate the system. Threat-response, belonging, and individuality processes are the interactions that create interrelatedness in the family system.

These processes are also differentiated. Though they are interdependent, threat-response, belongingness, and individuality processes are also unique from each other. A threat-response process that engages our nervous system to help us flee danger is different from reaching out to care for someone who is close to us. Having the ability to regulate our emotions allows us to maintain a sense of self while remaining connected to important others is also different from wanting to flee from danger. And providing care for someone close to us is different from regulating our emotions to respond in ways that are in line with long-term goals.

The three processes are also rule based. Across different systems we can see the unique steps or patterns that each of these processes follow. When our nervous system senses a threat, it sends signals throughout the body to respond to the threat. As described in Chapter 2, WPVA loops demonstrate the rules and patterns that emotion loops (threat-response process) take – monitoring the environment, seeing a potential stimulus, appraising it, and activating emotions in response. Emotion regulation loops (individuality process) also follow similar rules. Once the emotion loop is activated, our emotion regulation loop attends to it, evaluates it, and initiates a strategy to regulate it. The PANIC/GRIEF belonging process also follows rules. When we are separated from an attachment figure, we begin searching for that person. If the search proves unsuccessful, we fall into despair.

The attachment and triangulation processes also have rules. As described by Sue Johnson, there are five steps in the processes of the attachment system. We reach, and if we don't get the response we seek, we protest/or push or we may turn away/shut down. If this doesn't result in reconnecting, we go into meltdown. Similarly, the processes of a triangulation system follow a pattern. When there is tension, stress, or conflict between two people, we turn to a third person to help us regulate. The processes in the attachment and triangulation system can each be threat-response, belonging, or individuality processes.

Though these are broad rules that are often seen, they vary from family system to family system. Based on the sociocultural system the family is embedded in and whether they have privileges or experienced oppression, these processes may vary in intensity, frequency, and what is labeled healthy versus unhealthy. In addition, genetic, individual, attachment, and triangulation system difference will create variations in the process rule. For example, Sue Johnson talked about four types of patterns couples engage in based on their attachment system – criticize/withdraw, attack–attack, freeze and flee, and chaos and ambivalence. This is not only due to individual differences within each partner but also due to the triangulation patterns and sociocultural system in which the couple resides.

Threat-response, belonging, and individuality processes are also hierarchical. They are not hierarchical in that one is more important than another, but they are hierarchical in that they developed in an evolutionary order. Threat-response processes evolved first. All organisms have some form of fight, flight, or freeze threat-response processes. Mammals evolved belonging processes based on co-opting some of these responses. This way mammals care for their young, form attachments, and often live in social groups. Individuality processes evolved from threat-response and belonging processes. Those to which we belong can also pose a threat, therefore we need a way to be regulated how we respond to stay part of the group but also to support our survival. Through emotion self-regulation, we can be our self while being a part of a group.

These processes create boundaries – they determine who is in our family system and who is not. These processes are what make the behaviors within the family system different from those without. If we were to find out that our spouse cheated on us, the activation of the threat, belonging, and individuality processes would be unique from our response that would be activated if we found out that our neighbor's spouse cheated on them. In the former situation, it's likely that we would activate all three of these processes. In the latter situation, we most likely would not experience threat to our belongingness or individuality, but we may activate the belonging processes to provide more support for our neighbor. I would argue that the family system is unique because members can activate each of these processes simultaneously, and in many cases with greater intensity than other social interactions.

Finally, these processes are relatively stable across time. This is evident in the need for family therapy. Because these processes are relatively stable, they often have a hard time changing. Once rules are established in these processes, they get replicated repeatedly. If the environment stays the same, the family often has no need to change the rules of the processes. But as the environment shifts, if the family can't shift the rules of the processes, they often need outside help to do so. In addition, even though the rules of the processes change, the processes themselves often continue across time.

Is the Family an Autonomous System?

If we return to the question that started this chapter, I would argue that we have sufficient evidence to suggest that the family is an autonomous system. The three processes discussed here contribute to the generation and maintenance of the family system. These processes are interdependent, able to be differentiated, have rules, are evolutionarily hierarchical, determine who is inside the family and who is not, and are relatively stable. Therefore, the best available evidence points to the family being an autonomous system.

Chapter Recap

Autonomy can be defined in many ways – as having agency over what we do or owning one's beliefs and values and the behavior that stems from them. However, in family systems theory, autonomy has a different definition. Autonomy refers to the processes that generate and maintain the family system. Process is also a word that has a different definition in family systems theory. Processes are the interactions that create relatedness – they tie the people in the family system together.

Though there are likely more autonomy processes, the evidence points to three major process – threat-response, individuality, and belongingness. Threat-response processes are concerned with survival. Individuality processes are those that promote agency and ownership of one's behaviors. Belonging processes are those that promote connect to others. Each system that creates the family system exhibits these processes – though in different ways. These processes are also interdependent but can be differentiated from each other. These processes are also rule based and remain relatively stable across time.

> **Questions to Consider**
>
> 1. Based on the research summarized in this book and in this chapter, do you agree that the family is an autonomous system? Are there pieces of evidence that aren't discussed that would be important to consider when making this claim about the family?
> 2. Besides threat-response, belonging, and individuality processes, what other processes help generate and maintain the family system? What research would be needed to identify these processes?

Chapter 6

The Family as an Adaptable System

Does the evidence support the hypothesis that the family is an adaptable system?

Just like in the last chapter, let's revisit the idea of adaptation before drawing any conclusions. In Chapter 1, we relied on Bernd Rosslenbroich's concept of adaptation. He suggested that "adaptedness is a relational property of an organism or rather a property of the organism-environment system" (p. 230). Like autonomy, adaptation is often ambiguously defined. Often it is intertwined with the ideas of "fitness" when talking about evolution. Sometimes it is just thought of as change. To clarify what we mean when we talk about the adaptation, I want to turn to the source that Rosslenbroich used to talk about adaptation, *Foundations of Biophilosophy* by Martin Mahner and Mario Bunge (1997).

Drawing on the confusion that often accompanies the idea of adaptation, Mahner and Bunge described what they called the "Eight Senses of Adaptation." Each sense is differentiated from the other by a subscript number. But only seven of these senses are discussed here. Mahner and Bunge argue that the eighth sense of adaptation or adpatation$_8$ can be folded into the other senses of adaptation and they "disregard it henceforth" (p. 162).

Adaptation$_1$ is what is deemed universal adaptation. It is the idea that "a living being cannot exist separate from any habitat.... Hence, to say that an organism is adapted$_1$ amounts to saying that it is *alive in a given habitat*" (pp. 160–161). If a system can't exist in a habitat, it has failed to adapt, and therefore ceases to exist. Adaptation$_2$ occurs in the sensitivity processes of a system. A system will adapt based on the intensity of the stimulus. "An example is the adjustment of the eye to vision in bright or dim light" (p. 161). If the light is bright, the system adapts to allow for continued sight; a similar process happens if the light is dim.

Adaptation$_3$ refers to physiological changes in systems. This type of adaptation may be reversible or irreversible.

> Humans and other mammals can adapt to higher altitudes by increasing the number of erythrocytes, which compensates for the decrease

in atmospheric oxygen (reversible) . . . Cuttlefish and some other animals may change color depending on their habitat (reversible). The head shape of water-fleas depends on the temperature of the way in which they develop; accordingly, there is a seasonal variation of head form, which is called cyclomorphosis (irreversible).

(p. 161)

The ability to have reversible and irreversible psychological changes is key for a system. The ability of a cuttlefish to change color depending on the environment affords it a greater likelihood of survival in a given environment.

Adaptation$_4$ refers to systems within the system that help it perform functions within a given environment. "Thus, fins are an adaptation$_4$ of some vertebrate with an aquatic mode of life, and the feet of head lice are an adaptation$_4$ enabling them to cling to human hair" (p. 161). A system within a system provides a functioning for responding to the environment within which the system resides.

Adaptation$_5$ refers to adaptations that are made in response to changes in the organism or by a change in the environment, or both. This adaptation is sometimes described as the state of adjustment of a system to its environment and allows for comparisons to be made between two or more systems' suitedness to an environment – this is called *relative adaptedness*. Certain systems may be better suited to an environment than others.

Adaptation$_6$ are features of a system whose role has contributed to the success of the system. "In common teleological and anthropomorphic parlance, adaptation$_6$ are features that have been 'designed by' natural selection 'for' a given role" (p. 162). Adaptation$_7$ is the evolutionary process by which adaptation$_6$ occurs. In other words, as certain features or traits of a system become "designed for" a given environment, the process of the development of this feature is adaptation$_7$ while the outcome is adaptation$_6$.

Adaptation in the Family System

If the family is an adaptable system, then the evidence should show that the family has some if not all of the senses of adaptation. In other words, the evidence should be able to answer the following questions:

- Is the family alive in its given habitat?
- Does the family have sensitivity processes that allow it to adjust given the intensity of a stimulus?
- Does the family experience physiological changes? And are some of these physiological changes reversible or irreversible?

- Are there systems within the family system that help it perform functions within a given environment?
- Are some family systems better suited for the environment than others?
- Are there features of the family system that seemed designed for the environment, and did these result through the process of natural selection?

Is the family alive? The simple answer to this question is "yes." Even though there have been many who have warned about the "break down" of the family, the family system is still the most common and basic relational system. The notions that the family is ending or breaking down are typically couched in narrow and prescribed notions of what a family "should be" or "has been" in the past. Marriage historian and author, Stephanie Coontz addressed this idea in her 2016 article, *The Way We Never Were*. She argues that many people have referred to the 1950s as the golden age of the family and marriage. But, as she notes, this time was a "short-lived invention and that during its heyday, rates of poverty, child abuse, marital unhappiness, and domestic violence were actually higher than in the more diverse 1990s." She added that the same held true in 2016. Though the age of marriage has been increasing and there is greater diversity in what constitutes "family," Coontz argues that these trends are not the end of the family, but the results of the family system adapting to its environment.

Does the family have sensitivity processes that can adjust to intensity? As summarized in the previous chapters, the family has many systems and processes that allow it to adapt to the intensity of a stimulus. Threat-response, belonging, and individuality processes can be activated based on the intensity of stimulus or other factors in the environment. The extremes of this were described in Matthew Desmond's work on those facing eviction in Milwaukee. If a threat is extreme, the belonging process is activated "through a kind of accelerated and simulated intimacy" (p. 1321). As he described in his observations, the belonging process can be sensitive to the intensity of a threat. If the threat is extreme, like not knowing where you are going to live or provide food for your family, to survive, the belonging processes move with great intensity to create connections quickly, even if these relationships are fragile and only exist for a short time.

The same can be said for the other processes. If a partner discovers that their significant other is having an affair, the threat-response and individuality processes may engage based on who the partner was cheating with. As summarized earlier, affairs that occur with close friends tend to be more destabilizing to the family system than affairs with lesser acquaintances (Labrecque & Whisman, 2019). Each of the processes of the family system can adapt to the intensity of the situation.

Does the family system experience physiological changes? Threats and stress create physiological changes in the body. When we sense a threat in our environment, the brain initiates a pattern of events. One of the main steps it takes is the activation of the hypothalamic-pituitary-adrenal (HPA) axis. When a threat is present in the environment, the hypothalamus of the brain signals the pituitary gland to produce a hormone. This hormone signals the adrenal glands to increase the production of cortisol. Cortisol is the hormone that provides us with enough energy to deal with an extended threat. In addition, cortisol helps regulate the immune system and reduces inflammation. When there is a threat in our environment, our bodies need to be prepared to respond to a potential injury, so by increasing the immune and inflammation response, our bodies are ready to respond if injury should occur. Once the threat is dealt with, a new signal is sent from the hypothalamus, to the pituitary glands, and then to the adrenal glands to return to normal levels of production. This is an example of a reversible change that occurs in members of the family system.

However, if a person is under constant threat, some of the reversible changes may become permanent. In the short term, higher levels of cortisol are good for survival and can help us adapt to threats. However, if we are under a state of constant threat, or if we are having to turn our threat-responses on and off multiple times, this can result in what is referred to as allostatic load.

> Allostatic load refers to the price the body pays for being forced to adapt to adverse psychosocial or physical situations, and it represent either the presence of too much stress or the inefficient operation of the stress hormone response system.
>
> (McEwen, 2000, pp. 110–111)

Constant stress results in higher baseline of stress hormones in our body – our bodies adapt to the "load" of additional stress. But this process occurs across time, and sometimes becomes irreversible and without medical intervention, it may result in the development of diseases.

Researchers have suggested that a similar process may be replicated throughout the family system. Tamara Afifi, Anne Merril, and Sharde Davis (2016) proposed the concept of "relational load" to describe this process at a family level. Through their Theory of Resilience and Relationship Load they propose that:

> Family members who have more of a communal orientation toward stress . . . are likely to invest in their relationships and build emotional reserves through repeated communicate maintenance strategies. When people have positive emotional reserves, they then likely

appraise relationally stressful situation from a broader mindset and use communication patterns that uplift their partner and preserve the relationships. . . . Couples/family members who lack investments, and/or whose standards or expectations for investments are unmet, are likely to engage in more threatening appraisals and conflict behavior when they are stressed. . . [which] are likely to deplete a person's cognitive, emotional, and relational resources and exacerbate the stress.

(p. 665)

They argue that if this depletion occurs over a long period of time it can wear down the relationship, just as stress wears down the body, resulting in relational load. The relational load a system carries can leave its members at greater risk of mental and physical health problems.

The physiological and emotional load that a family system carries, though reversible at first, can become irreversible, requiring outside intervention. Similar to the cuttlefish which changes its color in an environment, as the family changes its interactions during stress, it may help them adapt to current stresses. But if the stress is constant, these short-term changes may become patterns that can lead to problematic functioning.

What systems help the family system function within an environment? While it could be argued that all of the systems within the family system help it function in a given environment, I want to focus our attention here on the attachment and triangulation systems. I would argue that the attachment and triangulation systems are similar to a dolphin's fin. Fins help dolphins survive in an aquatic environment, just as attachment and triangulation help humans survive in a social environment. Attachment relationships teach us how to be in a social world. If we are in an attachment system that is responsive, safe, and predictable, we often assume that the social world operates in this way. In addition, when the world isn't this way, we have a safe, responsive figure to help us deal with the unpredictability.

Triangulations system also help us survive in a social world. To survive in a social world, we need more than one person to whom we are connected. Changes in the environment, or the addition of new attachment system members through birth or other relationship formation, requires us to learn how to navigate the individuality and belongingness in relationships. The triangulation system is key to this process. When others enter our attachment relationships, it requires us to learn how to adapt to their presence. This is the "powerful influence" that Dallos and Vetere (2012) talked about in the summary of triangulation research. Triangulation can teach us how to stabilize attachment relationships, how to regulate emotions in the face of belongingness and individuality, and how to establish and maintain multiple relationships.

Are some family systems better suited for the environment than others? This is often where people again make arguments about what families *should be*. They may say that a certain family structure is "right" or "better" than another. However, the research doesn't bear this out. Families with gay and lesbian parents, transgender or non-binary parents, single-parent families, grandparent-headed families, and many other family structures can and do include families that are well suited to their environment. They can thrive in the face of adversity and respond to stress in ways that help strengthen and maintain the system (e.g., Dziengel, 2012; Farr, Bruun, & Patterson, 2019; Hsieh, Mercer, & Costa, 2017; Titlestad & Robinson, 2019).

Regardless of the makeup of the family, it is the processes that occur in the family that allow them to be better suited for the environment. If the attachment system is full of processes that allow for people to reach and reconnect, if the family can respond to stress in the balanced way described by Olson et al. (2019), or if the members of the family have emotion regulation strategies that include acceptance, reappraisal and problem-solving, they are likely to have less allostatic and relational load.

This idea was further emphasized by Tamara Afifi and her colleagues (2018). During the great recession of 2007–2009, they wanted to explore how economic hardship affected families. Research has shown that economic hardship can stress families and generate more conflict (e.g., Conger & Elder, 1994; Neppl, Senia, & Donnellan, 2016; Seccombe, 2002). Yet they found that the processes that existed in the families were more indicative of the families' outcomes than just the stress that resulted from economic hardship (Afifi et al., 2018). Summarizing this work, Afifi and her colleagues (2016) noted that some families "uplifted each other, were unified in combating the recession, were present emotionally and communicatively, and blamed outside forces (e.g., government, banks, great recession)" (p. 664). These families were more likely to bounce back following a large environmental stressor. Other families, "became stuck in intractable cycles of conflict where they perceived each other as a threat and communicated in ways (e.g., criticism, contempt) that preserved the self rather than the other person or the relationship" (p. 664). These families were more likely to break up through divorce or conflict. The patterns that were already occurring in the families' threat-response, belonging, and individuality processes were exacerbated by an outside stressor. In other words, it is processes, not family makeup, that determines whether a family is more suited to a given environment.

It should be noted, however, that some environments are so hostile to families that the processes that a family has won't be enough to sustain them during stress. If the family is embedded in a sociocultural system that marginalizes, dehumanizes, or uses violence to oppress them, the resilience built into the processes would likely be overwhelmed. Some might argue that this would just reflect "survival of the fittest," when, in reality, if any family system, regardless of structure, race, sexual orientation, gender identity, or religion would be strained and not be able to survive in such an environment.

Are there features of the family system that seem designed for the environment? Did these result through natural selection? We have strong evidence of the process of natural selection in almost all systems of the family system. Much of this evidence comes from our evolutionary ancestors or cousins. Most if not all animals have nervous systems that have fight, flight, or freeze responses; and, as Stephen Porges and Jaak Panksepp have suggested, all mammals have emotional and social engagement systems. Attachment systems have been observed in all mammals, and when mammals such as elephants experience a breakdown of these systems they experience many of the same reactions humans do (Bradshaw, Schore, Brown, Poole, & Moss, 2005). Though there is less recent research, Kerr and Bowen (1988) used examples of triangulation systems that have been observed in hens, lizards, and primates and argued that triangles were naturally occurring system.

Though these systems may not be optimally designed for our environment, they have, and are currently being shaped by the environment. Systems take many generations to evolve, so in many cases the family system as presently constituted was designed for a much different environment than it exists today. I would suggest that the lag of adaptation contributes to some of the difficulties that families face today. The individual, attachment, and triangulation systems may not be optimally designed for our current environment, but this like optimal design doesn't suggest the absence of adaptability but rather the slow process of natural selection.

Is the Family an Adaptable System?

If we use the criteria of Mahner and Bunge to evaluate the evidence, we have strong evidence to suggest that the family is an adaptable system. Systems and processes within the family system can respond based on the intensity of a threat or other stimulus. These systems and processes result in physiological changes that can be reversible or irreversible, and they help families perform necessary functions to survive. Some patterns of processes in the family system are more suitable to the environment than others. And though not totally determined by genes, evolution, or natural selection, the systems and processes of the family system are products of these forces. The current evidence supports the idea that the family is an adaptable system.

Chapter Recap

Adaptation can be understood as having seven senses. These include being alive in an environment; being able to react based on the intensity of a stimulus; make physiological changes based on a stimulus – these changes may be permanent or reversible; having systems that help an organism survive in a given environment; making changes in the environment, in the system, or both; has features that have evolved to help the survival of an organism; and the evolution of certain features seem "designed" for a given environment.

The family system meets each criterion of adaptation. There is sufficient evidence that suggests that the family system is alive, it can adjust to intensity, and it has systems within it that evolved to promote its survival. Research also suggests that the family system makes changes that are reversible or irreversible. The evidence points to supporting the hypothesis that the family is an adaptable system.

Questions to Consider

1. Based on the research summarized in this book and in this chapter, do you agree the family is an autonomous system? Are there pieces of evidences that aren't discussed that would be important to consider when making this claim about the family?
2. Are there other senses of adaptation that you believe should be considered? What are they? Why might they be important to the family system?

Chapter 7
Family Systems Theory Revisited

Now that we examined the evidence and applied it to the family systems theory hypotheses, let's pull it all together and provide a clear, succinct statement of what family systems theory is:

> *Family systems theory predicts and explains how people within a family interact, and how these interactions are different from interactions outside the family. The family system is created by the genetic, individual, attachment, and triangulation systems and is shaped by the sociocultural system in which the family is embedded. Each of these systems, and the family system are autonomous – they have processes that generate and maintain the system; and adaptable – they sense stimuli in the environment and within the family system to make reversible and irreversible changes based on the intensity of the stimulus. Autonomy and adaption in the family system are created by at least three processes – threat-response, belonging, and individuality. These processes, though unique, are interdependent, follow patterns or rules, and together create the unique interactions of the family system.*

This statement is different from previous descriptions of family systems theory but based on the evidence that we've examined thus far, I would argue that each claim that is being made is supported by evidence. But is this definition useful? Sometimes, theories are useful just "in theory" but come up short in practice. When they are applied to real-world situations, the proposals don't hold up.

Many books on family systems theory and family therapy use case examples to illustrate the author's claims and how they make sense for actual couples and family. Even when case examples are drawn from therapists' experiences, the richness of the family and the processes can be lost, as the family is being filtered through the author's lens. The same holds true for me. I want to use a case example to illustrate what I believe is the practical utility of family systems theory. To create the case example presented here,

I've drawn on experiences I have had with families in therapy. The family described isn't a "real" family; rather it is an amalgam of experiences taken from many families I have worked with. Just like other authors who use case examples to support their claims, I am drawing attention to details in this family that are the very things that would support the claims I'm making. As such, I don't see this case example providing any sort of empirical evidence for the claims made in this book. But I still think that this can be a useful exercise to demonstrate how this evidence could be gathered. I want to use a case example of a family to make an argument for the potential "real world" applicability of family systems theory. In other words, I want to demonstrate how family systems theory defined here can be used to explain interactions in a family.

Case Example

Carolina and Asha have been together for 20 years and married for five. They have a daughter, Raven, aged 17. Raven has been breaking curfew on weekends to drink, smoke pot, and hook up with her boyfriend. Carolina and Asha have done everything they can to get her home on time and to stop her risky substance use behavior. In addition, Asha is trying to cope with the recent death of her father. As the oldest of three siblings, she felt it was her responsibility to take care of her mother. Carolina has become increasingly frustrated with Asha. She feels that Asha's attention should be at home on their daughter who is struggling, not on her mother.

What would family systems theory help us explain about this family? Let's start by examining Carolina's and Asha's relationship. Their attachment system has fallen into a pursue-withdraw pattern. The role each partner takes in this system stems in part from their emotional regulation strategies. Carolina commonly uses problem-solving to deal with uncomfortable emotions. When her PANIC/GRIEF system is activated by recognizing tension through her social engagement system, she typically tries to modify the situation by trying to find ways to "fix" the problem. For her part, Asha tends to use an avoidance emotion regulations strategy. When she sees Carolina about to bring up some way to make their relationship better, this activates her FEAR system. She feels like running away, but because that's not an option, she suppresses her emotional response and tries avoiding her emotions.

The sociocultural system also has a large effect on this couple and their attachment system. As a Latinx woman, Carolina gets paid substantially less in her digital marketing job, yet she is unaware of this fact since the company has a policy that does not disclose the salaries of its employees. If she were making the same amount as her white, male colleagues, the family would be able to hire someone to help with Asha's mom. Asha is a teacher, and though this position provides health care, the state recently passed legislation that stripped the collective bargaining rights for her teachers' union and reduced the pension she would get when she retires. The stress that comes from the pressures both women feel at work adds to the tension of their pursue-withdraw pattern.

Not only do they feel the financial stress from their job affect their relationship, but they also live in a state where many people see their marriage as wrong. They are active in their church, but many churches in their community openly preach that gay and lesbian relationships are harmful for children. Many of Raven's friends in the past have parents who attend these churches that deem their relationship as sinful, and as such wouldn't not allow their children to come over to Carolina and Asha's home. This has also increased pressure on their attachment system as they sometimes feel the need to show that they are "good" and "normal" parents.

This stress on the attachment system has led to the formation of emotionally harmful triangles in the family. Often to avoid the tension that exists in their attachment system, Carolina and Asha focus their attention on Raven. Raven, feeling this tension, has begun being less and less open with her parents and turning more and more to her boyfriend. When Carolina and Asha found out about the boyfriend, on a night that they found Raven sneaking out, they became even more concerned and focused more and more energy on how to control Raven's behaviors.

During this same period, Asha's dad died. Asha grew up in a very enmeshed but rigid household. When Asha came out, her father was angry. Since that time until his death, the relationship between Asha and her dad was strained. Given the stress between her and Carolina and the stress in the triangle between her, Carolina, and Raven, Asha focused her energy on taking care of her mother. Asha and her mother's attachment system has always been one that was safe and predictable. Even though she is taking care of her mom's physical needs, it also gives her time to talk with her mother about the stress that is going on with Carolina and Raven. This had led to Asha's mother sometimes questioning the relationship between Carolina and Asha.

These two triangles reinforce and shape each other. When stress from either within or outside the family is heightened, Asha pulls closer to her mother and further away from Carolina. As Carolina feels Asha pulling away, she tries to draw her in by talking about issues with Raven. Though Carolina and Asha can talk about Raven, because they are avoiding or trying to fix the emotional disconnect in their attachment system, the conversations require that they focus more intently on what Raven is doing wrong. The more emotion that is put into trying to solve the "problem" with Raven, the more Raven pulls toward her boyfriend and away from her parents. As Raven pulls away, this stresses Carolina and Asha's attachment system, leading Carolina to pursue more closeness and Asha to turn toward her mother for comfort.

This has resulted in a family system that is chaotically disconnected. In each attachment and triangulation system, the threat-response processes are on high alert. To adapt to the stress, the belonging and individuality processes in each system that creates their family become problematic. It's not problematic that Raven would want to spend time with her boyfriend, or explore her identity outside the family, but because she fears the losing of her individuality as part of the triangle that she is in with her mothers, she engages in an attachment system that while reassuring now, could have problematic consequences. It's not problematic for Asha to take care of her mother or to have a close relationship with her, but it might be problematic if the triangle that exists between her, her mother, and Carolina serves to stress Asha and Carolina's attachment system.

This family is an autonomous system. It has processes that are generating and maintaining the system. The emotion regulation, attachment, and triangulation systems of this family are all generated by threat-response, individuality, and belonging systems. These processes are activated in response to the racism, sexism, and homophobia that exists in the sociocultural system and to the stress resulting from the death of Asha's father. This family is also an adaptable system. In response to stress that is happening inside and outside of the family system, the systems have responded. Given the need for belongingness in the face of threat, Asha is returning to a safe attachment system, but is creating a potentially problematic triangle. A similar process is happening with Raven. But instead of the need for greater belongingness, Raven's individuality processes are activated to push for relationships outside of her family.

The Limitations of Family Systems Theory

The previous chapters of this book have been spent outlining the case for this description of family systems theory provided earlier. Evidence has been provided to support the hypothesis that the family is an autonomous and adaptable system. I've also demonstrated, using a case example, that family systems theory may have real-world applicability. Yet, with all this evidence, I think that it is important to highlight some of the limitations and weaknesses of what has been proposed. No theory is ever complete. Though some theories, such as evolution or atomic theory, have so much evidence that they are considered scientific fact, this doesn't mean that there isn't still much to study and learn. As Jerry Coyne noted:

> A theory become scientific fact (or a "truth") when so much evidence has accumulated in its favor – and there is no decisive evidence against it – that virtually all reasonable people will accept it. This does not mean that a "true" theory will never be falsified. All scientific truth is provisional, subject to modification in light of new

evidence. There is no alarm bell that goes off to tell scientists that they've hit on the ultimate, unchangeable truths about nature.

(p. 16)

To make a theory better, it needs to be scrutinized and criticized. So, I want to spend the remainder of this chapter discussing some of the limitations of family systems theory and some of the "new evidence" that could come about regarding family systems theory. I want to highlight arguments against what has been proposed and examine those arguments. In addition, I want to make a case that family systems theory is an important and viable theory even with its limitations.

Is the Family Really Unique?

One of the main assumptions that the family systems theory rests on is that the family is a unique system. Family systems theory assumes that interactions within the family system are different from interactions that take place outside the system. But is this the case? In other words, are family relationships really unique? Do we need to be connected to family members or do we just need any type of connection?

There is much research that looks at social support and its effects on health and well-being. Social support is the idea that a person perceives their relationships as accessible and that they are cared for and valued in their social circles (Cohen, 2004; Cyranowski et al., 2013). Social support is a broader idea than a family system. When people study social support, they typically aren't concerned with specific relationships, rather they are concerned with whether people feel connected to anyone.

Meta-analytic studies of social support have found consistent associations between social support and well-being. Po Sen Chu and colleagues (2010) examined 246 studies exploring association between social support and well-being for children and adolescence. Overall, their analysis suggested a small association between social support and well-being. Similarly, Tayebeh Fashihi Harandi and colleagues (2017) used 64 studies to examine the association between social support and well-being on the mental health of adults. They found a moderate association between social support and mental health. Meta-analyses have also found links between greater social support and better sleep (Kent de Grey, Uchino, Trettevik, Cronon, & Hogan, 2018), and between greater social support and lower levels of inflammation (Uchino et al., 2018). Social support is an important aspect for health across the lifespan and in multiple domains. Loneliness is also a predictor of well-being and health. Like studies on social support, meta-analyses show that loneliness is associated with coronary heart disease, stroke (Valtorta, Kanaan, Gilbody, Ronzi, & Hanratty, 2016), dementia (Penninkilampi, Casy, Singh, &

Brodaty, 2018), chronic physical conditions in children and adolescence (Maes et al., 2017), and all-cause mortality (Rico-Uribe et al., 2018).

The analyses represent hundreds of studies and hundreds of thousands of people. Each of the findings is suggesting the importance of social connection. When we are connected, we are healthier and happier; when we are disconnected, we are sicker and sadder. But these studies aren't examining whether certain types of connections are more important than other. They are assuming that all connections have, more or less, the same amount of importance. It's not about who we are connected to, but the fact that we are connected that matters.

It could be argued that these findings are undermining the assertion that the family is unique. They are pointing to the fact that belonging and individuality processes happen outside of the family. It could be further argued that one doesn't need to feel connected to a family to have healthy belonging and individuality processes. In other words, it may be that the interactions that happen within the family system are not different from interactions happening outside of the system.

While this could be the case, I think it's important to push back on this claim, at least a little bit. One of the main limitations of loneliness and social support research is that it asks broadly about social connections. People aren't asked to specify who they are connected to and who matters most. Research that I have conducted with my colleagues Sarah Woods and Tara Roush explored if support in specific relationships matter than others. In 2014, we published results of a study that asked participants about support in different types of relationships. We looked at how emotional support with friends, romantic partners, and other family members were differentially associated with mental and physical health. With a sample of 1,321, we found that while romantic and family relationship emotional support was linked to health outcomes, reports of friend relationships were not linked to these outcomes, suggesting that support from partners and family members may matter more than support from friends to health.

But this is just one study. If we really want to say that the family is unique, we need more evidence. There is ample evidence showing the importance of family and romantic partners relationship processes on health or well-being for children and adults (e.g., Umberson & Thomeer, 2020); however, the research we have usually isn't comparing the effects of family and romantic partners to other aspects of social support. Moreover, as highlighted by Sarah Woods and her colleagues (2019), when studying adult health and relationships, we tend to only focus on the romantic partner and exclude other family relationships. Research that she, Patricia Roberson, and I have conducted together shows that in many instances family relationships outside of marriage potentially have a larger impact on health than marital relationships (e.g., Priest et al., 2019; Woods, Priest, & Roberson, 2019). Similarly, when studying children, we typically only explore the relationship they have with their parents, also ignoring other important relationships that they might have such as siblings or grandparents (Umberson & Thomeer, 2020). We need more research comparing multiple relationships from across social relationships to have enough evidence to say that the family is unique.

In addition, I'm extrapolating results from studies linking families' relationship processes to health outcomes to support assumptions that they weren't testing. I'm using these findings to suggest that families have larger effects on health and well-being because they can activate the threat-response, belonging, and individuality processes in unique and potentially extreme ways. Yet none of the studies set out to test this assertion. In other words, I'm speaking well beyond the data.

Family systems theory and family therapy research has, for decades, relied on the assumption that the family is unique. And I am as well. However, this assumption needs to be supported by more evidence. I think we need studies that observe unique interactions in family systems; we need studies that show that family interactions activate physiological processes in unique or extreme ways when compared to interactions with others; and we need these studies to include various family relationships that are often forgotten – siblings, grandparents, in-laws, among others. Until we have this data, we can only say that though the family system may be important, it may not be unique.

What About Connections Between Systems?

You'll notice that in the case study presented at the beginning of this chapter, I didn't extrapolate to what might be happening in the genetic, nervous, or other brain systems. Though it is likely that for any process to be activated in the family system, there are processes that must take place in every system within the family system, the research that could support this assertion has yet to be conducted. As I've detailed, we know that the nervous system responds to threats, and that the vagus nerve may help us stay socially engaged even when things are tense. We know that genes play a role in attachment systems, and we know that the brain has social systems that help it process social cues. But we don't know how this plays out in real time or across the life course. In other words, we don't yet have research that is able to examine the processes that occur in each system, and how they are activated and respond in real time when family interactions occur.

This points to another assumption that family systems theory is built upon, namely that the systems that create the family system are connected across generations and across development. Family therapists have for decades made this argument and built therapy models on this assertion. For example, writing in 2016, Monica McGoldrick noted:

> If we start with the most basic aim of therapy from a systems perspective, we might say it is to help clients make the best choices for their lives. And in order to make the best choices we human beings need to appreciate that we are all connected to each other and to the earth, to the past and to the future of each other and our planet ... It means, in effect, realizing that we are, to paraphrase Jorge Luis Borges, "the embodied continuance of those who did not live into our time (Borges, 1972, p. 21)" ... The context of understanding people, that is, the context of our belonging throughout our lives, includes the present context of our family and community, within the longitudinal context of our history, our present, and our future. It carries us all from birth and childhood through adulthood to death and defines our legacy for the next generation.
>
> (pp. 3–4)

However, much of this evidence I've summarized doesn't support this assertion made by McGoldrick. Generalizing the evidence to suggest that the systems are connected is problematic for at least two reasons.

First, most of the evidence on families often reflects short periods of time. Though some of the evidence I outlined is longitudinal in nature; it is often difficult to study how these systems are affected across time. What's more, studying families across generations is particularly difficult, as the family system tends to outlive researchers and specific research projects. Second, most of the evidence summarized only examines one system of the family system – not acknowledging how the interactions of these systems co-construct the family system. While some evidence has looked simultaneously at multiple systems, I am not aware of any research that looks at the genetic, individual, attachment, triangulation, and sociocultural systems simultaneously and much less each of those systems across generations.

This isn't a limitation unique to family systems theory. Many branches of science have had difficulty studying multiple systems and the connections between them, and I think family therapy researcher would do well to draw on how other disciplines have started to tackle this problem. One example of how addressing this limitation comes from developmental systems theory (DST; Witherington & Lickliter, 2016). As described by Susan Oyama, Paul Griffiths, and Russell Gray in 2001, DST:

> [i]s not a theory in the sense of a specific model that produces predictions to be test against rival models. Instead, it is a general theoretical perspective on development, heredity and evolution, a framework

both for conducting scientific research and for understanding the broader significance of research findings.

(pp. 1–2)

They further argue that the goal of DST was to move biology past the nature versus nurture debate. To do so they outline what they see as six themes of DST.

The first theme is joint determinism by multiple causes. Oyama and colleagues suggest that every trait of a system is produced by the interaction of many factors. They write:

> There are many influences on development, and there are many ways to group these interactions together. DST does not claim that all these sources of causal influence play the same role, nor that all are equally important . . . Rather, different groupings of developmental factors are valuable when addressing different questions.
>
> (p. 2)

DST theorists would argue that it is in the interactions of the systems that create the system where determinism occurs.

The second theme is context sensitivity and contingency. This theme suggests that the significance of a causal factor depends on the state of rest of the system. As summarized by Oyama et al., "Whenever a number of causal factors interact to produce an outcome, we should expect that the effect of changing one factor will depend on what is happening to others" (p. 3). They further suggest that many current biological frameworks encourage a search for genes that cause a certain trait; however, they see this as problematic, noting:

> As long as the DNA is thought of as containing information about developmental outcomes, it will seem sensible to inquire whether outcomes occur because they are represented in the chromosomes. Once an outcome is seen as an expression of genetic information that controls development, it acquires special status. It represents what the organism is "meant to be . . ." In such an intellectual framework, context sensitivity is often treated as interference with the basic pattern of biological causation. For DST, contingency is basic whether the results are expected or surprising.

DTS theorists would argue that there isn't one factor that causes any other factor; the context in which the system is embedded must be considered.

The third DST theme is extended inheritance. This theme suggests that a system inherits multiple resources that interact to create autonomy.

examine how this occurs across generations. But until then, it's important to acknowledge that this lack of evidence is another limitation of family systems theory.

Can Biology Explain Human Behavior?

The proposals and hypotheses of family systems theory outlined here have been largely reliant on concepts from biology. Autonomy, adaptation, and systems are all ideas that have specific biological meanings. Biology is built on the ideas of evolution and genetics. There have been many objections that have been raised about applying genetic and evolutionary ideas to human behavior. We can't go back in evolutionary history and see if our ancestors behaved a certain way, or how these behaviors may have changed across time. In addition, many have used the "idea of genetics" (not the actual science) to maintain power and oppress people based on what they see as "superior" and "inferior" genes.

This has resulted in three main criticisms leveled at evolutionary explanations for human behavior. First is genetic determinism. Genetic determinism is the idea that genes determine who we are and how we behave. In other words, when it comes to the nature versus nurture debate, those who apply evolutionary biological ideas to human behavior, some argue, are squarely in the "nature" camp. However, David Buss (2015), a developer of what is called Evolutionary Psychology, has pushed back on this assumption suggesting:

> Much of the resistance to applying evolutionary theory to the understanding of human behavior stems from the misconception that evolutionary theory implies genetic determinism. Contrary to this misunderstanding, evolutionary theory represents a truly interactionist framework. Human behavior cannot occur without two ingredients: (1) evolved adaptations and (2) environmental input that triggers the development and activation of these adaptations. Consider calluses as an illustration. Calluses cannot occur without an evolved callus-producing adaptation, combined with the environmental influence of repeated friction to the skin. Therefore, to invoke evolutionary theory as an explanation for calluses, we would never say "calluses are genetically determined and occur regardless of input from the environment."
>
> (pp. 16–17)

Buss is arguing that adaptations evolve to help an organism deal with the problems in the environment. Genes don't cause outcomes. Like calluses, we would never say that family processes are genetically determined and occur regardless of input from the environment.

The second criticism that often gets leveled against biological applications to human behavior is the idea that evolutionary theory suggests that human behavior can't be changed. Again, Buss argues:

> Knowledge about our evolved psychological adaptations along with the social inputs that they were designed to be responsive to, far from dooming us to an unchangeable fate, can have the liberating effect of paving the way for changing behavior in areas in which change is desired. This does *not* mean that changing behavior is simple or easy. More knowledge about our evolved psychology, however, dives us more power to change.
>
> (p. 17)

Buss returns to his example of the callus, suggesting that as humans we can make friction-free environments – like wearing gloves while doing work. This is a change that prevents the processes that result in callus. "Knowledge of these mechanisms and the environmental input that triggers their activation give us the power to decrease callus production" (p. 17). Again, I think the same sentiment applies to family systems. Family processes have rules for responding, and these rules are often very difficult to change. By understanding the rules and how they react in a given environment, more options for change become available.

The final criticism that is often leveled is that current adaptations are optimally designed. In other words, many assumed that if evolutionary explanations are to be believed, then humans and by extension the family, should be optimally designed for the environment. Again, Buss suggests:

> Because evolutionary change occurs slowly, requiring hundreds or thousands of generations of recurrent selection pressure, existing humans are necessarily designed for previous environments of which they are a product. Stated differently, we carry around a Stone Age brain in a modern environment . . . A strong taste preference for fat and sugar, adaptive in past environments, now leads to clogged arteries, Type 2 diabetes, and heart attacks. The lag in time between the environment that fashioned our mechanism . . . and today's environment means that some of our existing evolved mechanism may not be optimally designed for the current environment.
>
> (p. 18)

What is true of our appetites could be true of our family systems. The threat-response, belonging, and individuality processes have evolved over years and may not be optimally suited for the modern age. I would argue that this is why it is important for family therapist to understand the science of family systems theory. By understanding these processes, how and why they evolved, and that they may not be best suited for our current sociocultural system, we may be able to provide families with a better framework for change.

In addition, I think positioning family systems theory within other biological sciences helps lend credibility to the theory. By drawing on biological theories, we can show how our ideas are situated within the larger scientific community. If we create theories or assertions that aren't tied to the mainstream of scientific thought, it is likely that outside observers will disregard our ideas. By connecting the family system to biological systems, we create a direct line between the biological sciences and the study of families – creating a strong foundation for family systems theory.

The Future of Family Systems Theory

As I outlined in Chapter 1, there is a reciprocal relationship between theory and research. We use evidence to formulate a theory. The hypotheses of the theory are then tested through research. If the evidence continues to repeatedly support the hypotheses, then we can refer to these hypotheses as scientific fact. If the results of research do not support the hypotheses, then we must change or discard them. Also, in Chapter 1, I relied on Kerr and Bowen's assertion that, in 1988, research into understanding the family as a system "had barely scratched the surface," and I asserted that currently we have broken through the surface and "begun to dig into the core."

In the preceding chapters, I have endeavored to show that scientific evidence regarding the family system has "begun to dig into the core," and that the evidence supports the assertions that the family is an autonomous and adaptable system. In this chapter, I have outlined some of the limitations and unfounded assumptions of family systems theory. Given this, I would say that unlike the theory of evolution or atomic theory (Coyne, 2010), family systems theory *isn't* scientific fact. Like Kerr and Bowen, I see what I have outlined as a step in that direction. Then, as now, with new evidence and knowledge, the ideas presented thus far may need to change or be discarded. However, I do see value in continued exploration of the family as an autonomous and adaptable system. As I've argued in Chapters 5 and 6, I think the evidence is sufficient to make a strong case for the processes of autonomy and adaptation in the family system. With further research, the evidence for these hypotheses could become quite compelling.

I also think that these two organizing hypotheses can help move research away from "simply stating that a study is guided by a systemic perspective or family systems theory" and begin to build an even stronger base of support (Chen et al., 2017, p. 522). By refining family systems theory from more than 20 proposals, I believe that the theory has become more usable and testable. I have outlined specific autonomy and adaptation processes that, in my reading, are supported by the current evidence. I think research can and will discover other processes as well and come to learn more about how they interact through development and across generations. By focusing our research through family systems theory, I believe that we can dig deeper into the core. As we dig deeper, we may find robust and repeated evidence that the family is an autonomous and adaptable system. Through this process, like evolution and atomic theory, we may be able to eventually establish family systems theory as scientific fact.

Chapter Recap

The claim that the family is an autonomous and adaptable system is supported by much research. A case example of a family suggests that family systems theory might also have real-world applicability to explain and predict family interactions. But family systems theory isn't without its limitations.

Family systems theory rests on the assumption that the family is unique. It assumes that interactions that take place with family members are distinct and more important than other social interactions. Though family systems theory has relied on this assertion for decades, the body of evidence that supports this assumption is weak. More research is needed to determine if family interacts are indeed unique. If the research shows that this is not the case, then it would be better to generalize a systems theory that can describe any social interaction and not prioritize family interactions.

Family systems theory assumes that each of the systems within the family system and the environment that the family system is embedded interacts to shape the family system. It also assumes that these interactions unfold across time, are affected by the developmental trajectories of individuals, and span generations. While this may be the case, we currently don't have the evidence to support this assumption. Using frameworks such as developmental systems theory may be a way that researchers can begin to build this evidence needed to support this claim.

Family systems theory as presented here is also drawing on biological concepts to explain family interactions. The concepts of autonomy and adaptation are being borrowed from biological explanations in systems. Though many have critiqued biological explanation of human behavior, arguing that it can be deterministic, others have shown that biological and evolutionary explanations can and do provide a strong foundation for understanding humans and families. Specifically, David Buss's work in evolutionary psychology has sought to answer the criticism that are often levied at biological explanations of human behavior.

Given these and other limitations of family systems theory, we can't yet say that the hypotheses of family systems theory are scientific fact. But because family systems theory, as presently described, is more usable and testable than previous iterations, it could eventually have sufficient evidence to be considered fact. This will require researchers to systematically test and provide evidence for the hypotheses and claims of family systems theory, and family systems theory will need to be changed if the evidence contradicts it.

Questions to Consider

1. This chapter discussed some of the limitations of family systems theory. What are others you can think of? How could researchers address these limitations? Are there any limitations of family systems theory that you think would render it invalid?
2. How might researchers determine the real-world applicability of family systems theory? What are some of the barriers to conducting this type of research?
3. Do you agree that family systems theory could become scientific fact? Why or why not? What kinds of evidence would be needed beyond what we presently have to establish it as such?

Part 3

Linking Theory to Practice

Up until this point, there has been little discussion about psychotherapy and clinical intervention in this book. The focus has been on theory, not on practice. But family systems theory's utility has historically been in its clinical application. The reason we try to better understand family and human relationships is so we can alleviate relationship distress. In this last section, I want to talk about the role and importance of family systems theory to clinical practice. In doing so, my goal isn't to propose a new model or to advocate for the use of certain techniques. Rather my goal is to advocate for family systems theory as the best theory on which to position a family therapy practice. My goal is to argue that family systems theory provides family therapists with best foundation on which to do couple and family therapy.

To do this, I want to summarize two theories that researchers and family therapy model developers have positioned as better options to build a practice than family systems theory: the postmodern critique and attachment theory. Though there are other family therapy models that have been built on different theories such as cognitive behavioral family therapy, others have already detailed the limitations of building a psychotherapy practice on cognitive and behavioral theories (e.g., Dalal, 2018). I focus on postmodernism and attachment theory because the proponents of these ideas have made direct challenges to family systems theory and its hypotheses. I want to summarize these ideas and their strengths and limitations. Then, I make a case as to why I think the evidence suggests family systems theory is the best theory on which to build a practice.

However, I do this with a caveat: I'm not providing equal time. There have been hundreds of books and thousands of research articles written about postmodernism and attachment theory. In the next few chapters, I will only scratch the surface of these ideas. Despite this, I will make a case as to why family systems theory provides the strongest foundation for a building a family therapy practice, and why I think that it's important that family therapists investigate the evidence for themselves.

Then, I discuss how family systems theory can help us better understand clinical issues. The goal in discussing clinical issues is again, not to discuss how to intervene; rather it's to show how family systems theory can predict and explain the development and outcomes of clinical issues on the family system. While there are many clinical issues that could be discussed, I will apply this argument only to one area – trauma. Given the prevalence of trauma in many families, and the frequency with which families come to therapy to deal with trauma, I feel like this topic area serves as prime example of how family systems theory can explain how families strive to maintain autonomy and struggle to adapt when clinical issues are present. In the last decades, the researching and understanding of trauma and how they affect each system that creates the family system has increased. My goal is to summarize these findings and demonstrate that family systems theory can explain and tie together the science of trauma.

Another important issue in family therapy is model development – an issue I also address in this section. During the last decades, scholars have argued back and forth about model development. Some have concluded that family therapy is effective because of common factors that transcend models. Others have argued that model development is crucial to improve our practice. I argue that to improve practice, we need to first focus on improving theory. The more evidence we have for family systems theory, the better equipped we will be to improve our models.

Finally, the last chapter provides the summaries of the main arguments of this book and then provides two recommendations I think can help therapists and researchers keep family systems theory and family therapy vibrant. If we are going to have strong, scientifically valid theories that we can build impact family therapy models from, then as a field we need to do better. We need to read better and engage differently. Only by reading and engaging with science can we strengthen family systems theory and in turn provide better therapy for our clients.

Chapter 8

The Postmodern Critique and Family Systems Theory

Many recent advances in family therapy practice have been reliant on the postmodern critiques. The postmodern critique is built on ideas very different to the ones proposed here. Many postmodernists would reject the notion that accumulation of evidence can result in scientific fact. Rather, they would argue because humans continually interpret our experiences and our interpretations of those experiences, we can't have a unifying theory, nor can we have direct knowledge of the world. We can only know things through experience.

Postmodern writer and social theorist, John Shotter (1993) described postmodernism in the following way:

> A postmodernist approach to [world] requires us, first and foremost, to abandon the "grand narrative" of theoretical unity of knowledge, and to be content with more local and practical aims. This means abandoning one of the deepest assumptions (and hopes) of Enlightenment thought: that what is "really' available for perception "out there" is an orderly and systematic world (potentially) the same for all of us – such that, if we really persist in our investigations and arguments we will ultimately secure universal agreement about its nature.
>
> (p. 34)

Throughout this book, I predicated my arguments on a positivist (or postpositive) approach – the assumption that we can have direct knowledge of the world and develop a theory that can explain family relationships, even though we bring our own experience and assumptions to the research. Postmodern thinkers fully reject this idea. Through their critiques, they argue that it is impossible to have direct knowledge of the world, especially the social world.

The developer of postmodern family therapy models used the critique of postmodernism to develop their approaches. They, like other postmodernists, rejected a positivist approach. As Narrative Therapy developers

Michael White and David Epston (1990) wrote in *Narrative Means to Therapeutic Ends*:

> At the outset of the social sciences, social scientists, in an effort to justify their endeavor, to establish plausibility, and to lay claim to legitimacy, turn to the positivist physical science for maps upon which to base their efforts in the interpretation of events in social systems. When positivism – the idea that it is possible to have direct knowledge of the world – was successfully challenged, and when social scientists realized that other scientist proceeded by analogy, and that the analogies they were appropriating had already been appropriated elsewhere . . . they were free to turn elsewhere in their search for metaphors from which to derive and elaborate their theories.
>
> (p. 4)

Fundamental to postmodern models of family therapy is a rejection of obtaining knowledge of real world, and by doing so, rejecting the idea of the family as a system.

In *Exchanging Voices: A Collaborative Approach to Family Therapy* (2018), Lynn Hoffman argued that postmodernism requires a rejection of the idea of the family as a system, writing:

> The postmodern interpretive view proposes metaphors for our work that are derived mainly from criticism and the language arts. Since therapy is an art of conversation, these metaphors are close to home than the biological and machine metaphors we have been using. Their particular strength comes from the fact that they are non-objectivist and, at the same time, socially and politically sensitive.
>
> (p. 102)

Similarly, in *Conversation, Language, and Possibilities* (1997), Harlene Anderson describes how her work moves away from the systems concepts. She suggests that her approach moved from understanding relationships as a:

> [s]ocial system defined by role and structure to a system that is contextually based and a product of social communication; from a system composed of an individual, a couple, or a family to a system composed of individuals who are in relationship through language.
>
> (p. 4)

Anderson positions herself as being different from approaches rooted in systems that are autonomous and adaptable.

White and Epston also position themselves against the idea of the family as a system. They write:

> In regard to family therapy – which has been our area of special interest – the interpretive method, rather than proposing that some underlying structure or dysfunction in the family determines the behavior and interactions of family members, would propose that it is the meaning that members attribute to events that determines their behavior. Thus, for some considerable time I have been interested in how persons organize their lives around specific meanings and how, in so doing, they inadvertently contribute to the "survival" of, as well as the "career" of the problem. And in contrast to some family therapy theorists, rather than considering the problem as being required in any way by persons or by the "system," I have been interested in the requirements of the problem for its survival and in the effect of those requirements on the family members' cooperative but inadvertent response to the problem's requirements.
>
> (p. 3)

Each of these family therapists called for the abandoning of the positivist approach to family relationships and family therapy and that there were better ways to understand and explain the family than using the concept of "system." They argued that to make sense of our lives and our closest relationship we should focus on the meaning, language, and stories we use to describe those relationships.

In rejecting the positivist approach and the metaphor of "system," these family therapy innovators built their models on unique assumptions. Though each of the postmodern family therapist built their model on slightly different assumptions, I want to use those articulated by Harlene Anderson as they are clear and reflected in the writings of the other postmodern family therapy models. She built her approach on the following assumptions:

1. Human systems are language- and meaning-generating systems.
2. Their construction of reality is forms of social action rather than independent individual mental process.
3. An individual mind is a social composition, and self, therefore, becomes a social, relational composition.
4. The reality and meaning that we attribute to ourselves and others and to the experiences and events of our lives are interactional phenomena created and experience by individuals in conversation and action (through language) with one another and with themselves.
5. Language is generative, gives order and meaning to our lives and our world, and functions as a form of social participation.

6. Knowledge is relational and is embodied and generated in language and our everyday practices.

(p. 3)

As evident in this list, most postmodern family therapy approaches view language and experience as the important aspects of human relationships. The language we used to describe our experiences is what gives meaning to those relationships and how we see ourselves and others.

The Problems With Postmodernism

The focus on language and how it shapes and creates meaning to relationships is an important aspect of family and all other social relationships. And I would agree that language is also a key component of the process of therapy. I think that Hoffman, Anderson, White, and Epston and others' ideas about language and how it shapes social relationships is an important addition to family therapy models and practice. However, I disagree with the notion that we need to abandon a positivist framework of gaining knowledge about the world. For decades, scholars have argued against the postmodern assumption that direction knowledge of the world can't be obtained (e.g., Rosenau, 1991; Spiro, 1996); some have gone as far to argue that it is because of this stance postmodernism is "both useless and false" (Erwin, 1997). David Pilgrim (2000) spoke directly of how these critiques of postmodernism apply to family therapy in his article, The Real Problem for Postmodernism. In it he argues that postmodernism will fail family therapists, noting:

> My prediction about postmodernism failing family therapist is based upon a lack of confidence in its practical utility . . . In particular, I would draw attention to the strengths of postmodernism which are simply a continuation of, or are shared by, prior traditions it challenges.
>
> (p. 9)

He is suggesting that the best ideas of postmodernism were borrowed from other philosophical traditions. He continues to list multiple examples of how postmodernism borrowed ideas, but Pilgrim highlights one especially relevant for the arguments of this book:

> A final appeal of postmodernism is that it problematizes knowledge claims about reality. However, a range of . . . philosophers of science have encouraged scientist and non-scientist alike to approach knowledge skeptically. It is possible to embrace this skepticism without having to embrace postmodernism and abandon realism. Thus while

all postmodernists are skeptical of claims about reality, not all skeptics are postmodernists.

(p. 10)

Pilgrim is arguing, and I agree, that a positivist stance doesn't mean abandoning skepticism or criticism. I would argue that currently the process of proposing a theory with testable predictions, testing those hypotheses, and based on the evidence, accepting, rejecting, or tweaking our predictions is key to increasing knowledge – and this process requires skepticism and criticism. I have frequently used the theories of evolution and atoms throughout this book to make the case, but I think that the same can be said for theories of family relationship. I've proposed that family systems theory is the best theory to construct a family therapy practice. And I have laid out evidence that suggests strong support for the hypotheses of this theory. This is a method that most postmodernists would find fruitless.

Yet, in proposing their ideas, I would argue that they are proposing a theory with testable hypotheses. In pushing back against the idea of the family as a system and instead arguing that other analogies better describe families and social interactions, they are engaging in a positivist process. Throughout their writings, these authors are proposing ideas that can be and have been tested empirically. Harlene Anderson writes about how conversation invites belonging, arguing that "being responded to creates a sense of belonging and be connected" (p. 120). Much research on family communication studies and Olson's Circumplex Model supports this assertion. In other words, Anderson is making a claim that can and has been evaluated and supported.

Similarly, White and Epston argued "that the text analogy provides a frame that enables us to consider the broader sociopolitical context of persons' lives and relationship" (p. 27). To make this argument, he has placed value on different types of evidence – in this case the writings of Foucault. Yet, as I summarized in Chapter 4, the broader sociopolitical context of a person's life and relationships can be addressed through a theory with testable prediction – McNeil Smith and Landor (2018) do just that. Just like Anderson, White and Epston are making a claim that can be evaluated and supported. Though they are abandoning the idea that we can have direction knowledge of the social world, I would argue that their ideas can be studied and evaluated.

What's more, Anderson's model assumes that the mind is a social composition, and that language shapes our reality. As I summarized earlier, researchers have found more than 36 parts of the brain that are engaged during social interaction (Alcalá-López et al., 2018), and the mirror neuron system and the mentalizing system may be of especial importance to autonomy and adaptation (Vogeley, 2017). The field of sociolinguistics

(Chambers, 2007) uses the scientific method to test assertions about how language shapes our relationships and realities. Even though they are saying that we can't have direct knowledge of the world, the assertions these postmodern family therapists have put forward are being tested.

The Case for Family Systems Theory

It could be that the "text" analogy is a better foundation for a family therapy practice, but to know that would require a rejection of some of the core tenets of postmodernism. It would mean adopting a positivist framework. I think that a positivist framework is necessary for the continued advancement of family therapy. The process of accumulating evidence in support of a theory is currently the best method we have for gaining knowledge. This is evident in many other disciplines of science and this process has resulted in large medical and technological advancements. I think we can come to a scientific consensus about the best theory for explaining family interactions, and I would argue that we currently have strong evidence for using family systems theory to do so.

Though many postmodern family therapists abandoned the systems metaphor, in many cases they are still drawing on systemic ideas but just calling it different names. For many of these approaches, the important system is the language system. Even though they are talking about words, stories, and narratives, the goal is still to have stories that reduce their anxiety, acknowledge their individuality, and allow for belongingness. I see language as an important part of facilitating autonomy, adaptation, and the threat-response, belonging, and individuality processes. In other words, we can take the great ideas that Hoffman, Anderson, White, Epston, and others have suggested, without abandoning family systems theory.

Given these limitations and critiques, I would suggest that family systems theory provides a better foundation than postmodernism to build a family therapy practice. Since it uses a positivist framework to test its assertions, family systems theory can be directly challenged and scrutinized. It can change and become better based on new evidence. In addition, the "unique contributions" of postmodernism can be found in other disciplines (Pilgrim, 2000) and many of the ideas of postmodern family therapist can be better supported with the evidence we currently have. Family systems theory, therefore, can include the best parts of postmodern family therapy and still grow and change in response to new evidence.

Chapter Recap

Many of the advances in family therapy practice have come from postmodernism. Postmodernism rejects the idea that we can have a unifying theory of knowledge and argues instead that human systems are language- and meaning-making systems and that reality is a social process. Narrative therapy, collaborative language systems, and solution-focused therapy are all grounded in the postmodern critique and these assumptions. Though postmodernism has helped generate advances in family therapy, it falls short as a foundation to build a family therapy practice.

By rejecting a positivist framework, postmodernism comes up short. Many postmodern family therapists reject the idea of the family as a biological system; this rejection is not based on an examination of the evidence, rather it is often done by suggesting that we can't really make claims about reality. Yet, many postmodern family therapists have proposed theories and hypotheses – thus making claims about reality. In many cases these claims have been tested and can fit into family systems theory and the accompanying hypotheses. In other words, family systems theory can incorporate all the important advances brought about from postmodernism without having to abandon objective claims about reality and being a theory with hypotheses that can be proven false. As such, family systems theory provides a stronger foundation to build a family therapy practice.

Questions to Consider

1. Do you agree with the criticisms leveled against the postmodern critique? Are there other criticisms that you see as more important?
2. Which theory do you think provides a better foundation to build a therapeutic practice – the postmodern critique or family systems theory? What evidence do you have to support your argument?
3. Do you see a way to reconcile family systems theory and the postmodern critique? Or should we just choose one and abandon the other?

Chapter 9

Attachment Theory and Family Systems Theory

Sue Johnson echoes the critique I levied against postmodernism. In her book, *Attachment Theory in Practice* (2019), she writes:

> In order for clinicians to operate in an optimally efficient and effective fashion, we need a cohesive science-based theory that is capable of addressing emotional, cognitive, behavioral, and interpersonal dysfunction. This theory must apply across the modality of individual, couple, and family therapies, and it must offer three basics of any scientific endeavor: Systematic descriptions based on observation and the outlining of patterns; prediction linking one factor to another; and a general explanatory framework, which must be supported by a large corroborating body of research.
>
> (p. 4)

Like her work, this book is predicated on the idea that a cohesive, science-backed theory is needed to build a strong clinical practice. Even though Johnson and I agree in what is needed to build a good practice, we come to different conclusions on what theory best meets these requirements.

Sue Johnson argues, "I submit that there is only one candidate that comes anywhere near fulfilling these criteria, and that is the developmental theory of personality termed attachment theory, as outlined by John Bowlby" (p. 5). And she is not the only one. In their 2013 book, *Unifying Psychotherapy*, Jeffery Maganavita and Jack Anchin make a similar case. They lay out the evidence in the individual, attachment, and triangulation systems, and they make the case as to why attachment theory may be the best theory for unifying psychotherapy. But is that the case? Before I offer my points of disagreement, I want to summarize the core tenets of attachment theory. I have touched on some of the ideas of attachment theory and research in Chapter 3. But I want to revisit and outline the core assumptions of attachment theory to allow for a clear comparison with family systems theory.

Attachment theory centers on the idea of a secure base. If we have a predictable, safe connection with a close other, then we are more likely to explore our world and develop a sense of competence. The presence of a secure base can help us regulate our emotions – turning to someone who is responsive, safe, and predictable when we experience distress can help calm our nervous system. In addition, when we get separated from our secure base, we can experience distress, and we seek to reestablish contact with our secure base. Our experience with our secure base, or with those who we want to provide security but who don't, create mental models of how we respond in relationships. These working models can be relationship dependent – we can have a working model of one person as response and safe and another as unpredictable and unsafe; however, attachment theory proposes that most people have a persistent attachment style that is prominent in most of the important relationships.

Attachment theory also prioritizes togetherness. Sue Johnson see attachment theory as a bonding theory. She writes:

> Attachment is fundamentally an interpersonal theory that places the individual in the context of his or her closest relationships; it views mankind as not only essentially social but also as *Homo vinculum* – the one who bonds. . . . This theory is essentially concerned with emotion and the regulation of emotion, and it particularly privileges the significance of fear. Fear is viewed not only in terms of everyday anxieties, but also on an existential level, as reflecting core issues of helplessness and vulnerability; that is, as reflecting survival concerns regarding death, isolation, loneliness, and loss. . . . It is a developmental theory; that is, it is concerned with growth and flexible adaptiveness. Bonding theory assumes that the close connection with trusted others is the ecological niche in which the human brain, nervous system, and key behavioral patterns evolved and is the context in which we can evolve into our best selves.
>
> (p. 6)

Like the ideas presented in this book, attachment theory is concerned about threat-response processes – how we deal with vulnerabilities, survival, and loss, and with belonging processes – being connected is key to maintaining and generating close relationships. However, it views individuality processes as the result of successful bonding. Only when we have a secure base do we feel safe enough to explore our world.

The Insecurities of Attachment Theory

Attachment theory is not without its detractors. Some have argued that it "overpromises and under-delivers" (Aaron, 2016). In examining the research and hypotheses of attachment theory, Robert Ludwig and Martha Welch (2019) argued: "One must conclude that the attachment construct has not been the breakthrough . . . that Bowlby heralded it would be in 1960" (p. 27). The rationale and evidence for these conclusions is varied, and we don't have time to cover each of these criticisms; but I would encourage readers to explore and examine the critiques that these and other authors have made regarding attachment theory. I want to focus my critique on two areas – relationship complexity and the individuality processes. In doing so, I want to be clear that I agree that human bonding is important. As I've outlined, I see the attachment system as a key system in the family system, and belonging is a core process that creates that system. However, like Ludwig and Welch (2019), I think the explanatory ability of attachment theory is limited.

The Secure Base Problem

One limitation of attachment theory is its overreliance on a singular secure base – "a platform from which to move out into the world, take risk, and explore and develop a sense of competency and autonomy" (Johnson, 2019, p. 7). Attachment theory assumes that if a person has "a" secure base, they will develop an internal working model that allows them to approach relationships and emotional regulation in a healthy way. I find this problematic because it doesn't account for relationship complexity.

Relationships are dynamic and unfold across time. Just because a person is in an attachment system that is safe and predictable doesn't mean that this relationship will continue in the same manner. Both the interactions that occur in a relationship and the salience of the relationship can change across time. Holly Ruhl and her colleagues showed evidence of these types of changes in their 2015 study. They surveyed 273 teenagers across grades 6 through 12 and examined how the attachment relationship with parent changed across time. They found that across these six years, teens' relationships with their parent became more secure – the level of attachment avoidance and anxiety that teens reported with parents decreased between sixth and twelfth grade. In discussing these findings, these researchers offered a few suggestions for their findings. Of particular note was the idea that, "As adolescents develop more salient peer and romantic relationships, they may report more security with parents because they are less reliant on parents as source of relational fulfillment." In other words, though a teenager may have had an attachment system with a parent that was marked by insecurity, as the teenager develops and creates other relationships, they begin to experience the attachment system with their parents differently.

If this is the case, where is the secure base? Is it with a parent, with a friend, or with a romantic partner? If the parental relationship served to create the internal working model of attachment for these teens, then why did the relationship with the parents become more secure as other relationships gained greater importance?

To me, a better explanation for these findings is found in family systems theory. Though family systems theory views the attachment system as important, it also accounts for the process of triangulation. The triangulation system can better explain the results of Ruhl et al (2015). In this case, the attachment avoidance and anxiety are reduced not by a secure base, but rather through the introduction of new relationships. It may be that the base didn't become secure, rather through triangulation the system stabilized. The introduction of a new relationship stabilized a previously unstable dyad (Kerr & Bowen, 1988).

What's more, family systems theory better encapsulates other factors that can influence the attachment system. If you recall from Chapter 3, when researchers study multiple attachment relationships they find "shockingly" different results (Benware, 2013; Doyle et al., 2009; George et al., 2010). If we have a secure base or an internal working model of attachment that is created in childhood, then which attachment system is the most important? If I have an insecure attachment to my mother but a secure attachment to my father, then what will my internal working model be? Research has shown the interaction between parents and children only account for about 50% of the parent–child attachment relationship (Verhage et al., 2016); and researchers have further emphasized the role that genes play in attachment process (Golds et al., 2020). With all this considered, the idea of a "secure base" seems to fall apart. Regardless of how predictable and safe a romantic relationship or a parent–child relationship is, it doesn't mean that the attachment system will be secure, or that the person will develop a secure internal working model of attachment. Rather multiple relationships, individual and sociocultural factors, and genes are all going to influence our experience in relationships – factors that are accounted for in family systems theory.

The idea of a secure base also is problematic in that it puts the focus on a singular person to provide for our emotional well-being. I think that this can set people up for unrealistic expectations regarding relationships. We can't expect a singular person to be available to use every time we need them. Throughout the course of a relationship system, the availability of the person we rely on for emotional support is going to vary. As Esther Perel described it, "We expect one person to give us what once an entire village used to provide, and we live twice as long." If we expect one person to take on the role of the secure base for us, we are likely to be let down. What's more, parents don't have to get it "right" all the time for the attachment security to develop. In their study of low-income mothers and children, Susan Woodhouse and her colleagues (2020) found that as long as the mother held infants until fully soothed 50% of the time, these infants were likely to develop security in their attachment systems. In my view, getting it right half of the time doesn't reflect the idea of security that is often promoted by attachment theorists.

The idea of the secure base can also be problematic for the person that is supposed to provide the security. For example, Justine Gunderson and Anne Barrett (2017) examined what they called "intensive mothering" and how it affected a mother's well-being. Using a sample of 1,388 mothers, they tested how providing high levels of emotional support and high degree of thought and effort into their parenting effected depressive symptoms, self-rated mental health, and their positive and negative affect. They found that mothers who reportedly provided high levels of emotional support to their children had more depressive symptoms, worse self-rated mental health, and more negative affect. On the other hand, mothers who had greater thought and effort investments into their children had better mental health. These researchers noted, "Our findings are consistent with research reporting that mothers' sacrifice of their own needs and desired to engage with their children, regardless of their age, increases stress and reduces autonomy – both of which diminish emotional well-being" (p. 1005). In other words, it may be that if the mother is the only person providing a secure base for a child, this could be problematic for her own well-being – in other words, the creation of the secure attachment system may not be healthy for both members of the system.

I think family systems theory provides a more robust and sharper description of relationship complexity. Because family systems theory views the attachment system as an autonomous and adaptable system embedded in the family system, it can better account for development across time and provide better descriptions of how attachment systems influence each other and overlap, and it doesn't prioritize certain family relationships above others. Moreover, it doesn't need to reduce relationships to either secure or insecure. Rather, it allows for a dynamic, developmental interplay of autonomy and adaptation across multiple systems that create the family system.

What About Individuality?

The second issue I want to raise regarding attachment theory is its treatment of the individuality process. Attachment theory posits that we develop a sense of individuality only when we have a safe and secure base from which to explore the world. It sees individuality as the result, not a process of an attachment relationship. But is this actually the case?

As I described earlier, Jared Anderson raised concern about the forgotten role of individuality in his 2020 article, Inviting Autonomy Back to the Table. In it he summarizes research that shows the importance of individuality processes, noting that:

> Autonomy is an important ingredient in determining relationship functioning. Individuals with higher levels of autonomy are more open, less defensive, and engage in healthier communication strategies during disagreement and conflict with their partner. They are more responsive and encouraging, and less intrusive with their partner. This is predicted by theory, which suggests that higher levels of self-determination or ownership of behavior and action allow a person to be more open to other ideas, accept influence, be curious, and self-reflective, all key stance when engaging with your partner around differences and disagreements.
>
> (p. 10)

As I noted in Chapter 5, he is using autonomy not in the biological sense that I have used throughout this book; however, his argument is supported by evidence. Individuality is a key and important process in healthy relationship functioning.

I don't want to re-summarize the research that Jared Anderson uses to draw these conclusions, but I would encourage the reader to examine it. Rather, I want to focus on the theoretical question raised by Jared Anderson, "Does a secure attachment to an intimate partner provide the secure base that supports exploration and autonomy, or does greater autonomy allow individuals to more authentically and securely bond with their intimate partners" (p. 11). Anderson is noting what I've previously discussed – attachment theory posits that individuality is the result of a secure base. Only when we have a safe, responsive, secure base are we able to explore the world. When a person gets distressed from exploring their world, they return to the secure base for comfort and that allows them to once again go out and explore.

He is then proposing an alternative. He is arguing, as others have (e.g. Schnarch, 2009; Ryan & Deci, 2017) that security in close relationships is a by-product of individuality. He writes,

> [I]f you are *solely* dependent on others (even you partner) for frequent validation and soothing in order to regulate yourself, then you will neither be self-determined nor feel truly secure. Your actions will be primarily motivated to maintain validation from your partner, thus acting in ways to please (or appease) them rather than acting in ways that are consistent with your values, are fully endorsed, and *owned*.
>
> (p. 11)

From this perspective, individuality processes promote secure belonging.

Anderson notes that we currently don't have research to strongly endorse either model. However, I would guess that even if we did research comparing processes, the answer to the directionality wouldn't be clear. My reasoning for this stems from the family systems theory proposal that the belonging, individuality, and threat-response processes are interdependent; and from the hypothesis that the family system is an adaptable system. Family systems theory wouldn't necessarily predict that one process creates another, rather that the autonomous and adaptative nature of the system would require certain processes to be more salient than others given the context of the environment and of the other systems within the family system.

It may be that in infancy, we may need stronger belonging processes, and in toddlerhood we may need stronger individuality processes. When we create a new romantic partnership, we may need stronger belonging processes; to sustain this relationship over time, we may need to place emphasis on individuality processes. During a crisis, one process may have greater activation than another; or during a developmental transition, the processes may need to be restructured. Yet, at each of these junctures, what is needed depends on genetic, individual, and sociocultural factors. In other words, relationships and the systems that create and influence them are too dynamic to have a linear test that examines whether a secure base creates individuality or that healthy individuality creates relationship security.

If we see the family system as a system that makes temporary and permanent changes, and as a system that responds to the intensity of a stimulus in the environment, then we can better understand how the individuality, belonging, and threat-response processes operate in the family. By doing research that focuses on all three processes, we can better understand how processes are activated when an adaptation is required. In other words, I think the question proposed by Anderson focuses on the wrong answer. To try to determine whether belonging begets individuality or if individuality begets belongingness misses the point. Family systems theory posits that relationships are made by both (and threat-response processes). A "healthy" family system will be able to activate these processes with different intensity when it is required. A "healthy" family system can adapt patterns of these processes to respond to stress. In these adaptations, the family maintains autonomy. Sometimes the changes the family makes will be permanent; at other times it will be temporary. Family systems theory doesn't expect or provide a linear answer, rather it proposes that autonomy and adaptation are key to family survival.

The problem with attachment theory's treatment of the belonging process is in the assumption of its linearity. In proposing that a secure base creates individuality misses the dynamic interplay of individuality and belongingness that occurs across time. Family systems theory doesn't propose a linear process. Rather it takes an adaptive stance. Threat-response, belonging, and individuality processes vary in their intensity across time. These processes may make temporary or permanent changes depending on what supports the autonomy of the system.

The Case for Family Systems Theory

Given these issues with attachment theory, I would argue that family systems theory provides a better foundation for understanding human relationships and building a family therapy practice. Family systems theory accounts for the complexity of relationships in ways in which attachment theory does not. Family systems theory provides a clearer conceptualization of the interdependence of the belonging and individuality processes. Because of its focus on adaptation, it can escape the black-and-white thinking of security versus insecurity. Instead it can explain why relationship processes change across development and how varying constellations of these processes can serve to promote the autonomy of the family system. I would argue that family systems theory allows for therapists to build a practice that creates more avenues for addressing relationship distress. Though attachment systems are key to the family system, by downplaying other processes and other systems, attachment theory misses the mark.

Chapter Recap

Many have argued that attachment theory provides an evidence-based theory on which an effective family therapy practice can be built. Researchers have spent decades testing the assumptions of attachment theory and have found some strong evidence. Yet, attachment theory has some major limitations about explaining family relationships.

One limitation is the concept of a secure base – a relationship that serves to be the one from which we go out and explore our world. This concept assumes that when we have a secure base, we develop an internal working model about the way we approach relationship. However, research has found that attachment relationships can vary widely. In other words, people don't just have one attachment relationship, but they are embedded in multiple attachment relationships throughout the course of their lives. As such, we don't have a singular secure base from which to explore the world. Instead the multiple attachment systems influence each other and our internal working model of relationship. By relying on the concept of a secure base, attachment theory does a poor job explaining why attachment systems can vary so widely in their processes and neglect to see the effect of triangulation on family relationships.

Another limitation is how attachment theory treats the individuality process. Attachment theorists would suggest that individuality stems from the secure base. Only when we have a secure base to return to do we feel safe enough to explore the world around us. However, individuality and belonging processes are linear – one doesn't create the other. In proposing that a secure base creates individuality misses the dynamic interplay of individuality and belongingness that occurs across time. Family systems theory provides a better explanation for these processes since it doesn't take a linear stance. In family systems theory, adaptation in these processes is key – threat-response, belonging, and individuality processes vary in their intensity and importance across time.

The ability of family systems theory to better describe relationship complexity gives it an advantage over attachment theory. Family systems theory can see the importance of attachment systems but doesn't needlessly prioritize a secure base. In family systems theory, all relationships influence the individual and the other relationships. The salience of relationships can also change across time. In addition, family systems theory doesn't prioritize belongingness over individuality. It sees both processes, along with the threat-response processes, as interdependent and adaptive across time.

Questions to Consider

1. Do you agree with the criticisms leveled against attachment theory? Are there other criticisms that you feel have been left out that could be added?
2. Do you agree with the assertion that family systems theory provides a better foundation than attachment theory to build a therapeutic practice? Why or why not? What evidence do you have to support your argument?
3. What are the strengths of attachment theory that are not present in family systems theory? Could family systems theory incorporate these strengths?

Chapter 10

Trauma in Family Systems Theory

Another advantage of family systems theory is how it can conceptualize and add context to clinical problems. I would argue that family systems can provide a better research-based understanding of clinical issues than either the postmodern critique or attachment theory. Though postmodernism and attachment theory provide context to clinical issues, family systems theory ties together disparate research and shows how common clinical issues disrupt the family system through autonomy and adaptation.

This is readily apparent when examining the research on trauma. As Charles and Kathleen Figley (2009) argued, "Trauma is by nature interpersonal and is, therefore, a systemic entity" (p. 173). Trauma effects and is affected by genes, the brain, body, and emotions, attachment relationships, triangles, and the family and sociocultural systems. This is done through the threat-response, belonging, and individuality processes that create autonomy and adaptation in family system. In this chapter, I want to briefly summarize research on trauma and how it affects the genetic, individual, attachment, triangulation, family, and sociocultural systems. I also want to show how the individuality, belonging, and threat-response processes, and a system's ability to adapt is affected by trauma. I do this to show how family systems theory can provide a comprehensive and contextualized theory for understanding trauma effects and is affected by the family system.

What Is Trauma?

In discussing trauma, David R. Grove, Gilbert J. Green, and Mo Yee Lee (2020) wrote:

> Trauma can occur when a person finds themselves in a situation in which they fear they may die or experience serious injury or sexual violence. The trauma can result from a person directly having the experience, witnessing the experience, or learning about a person close to them have the experience.
>
> (p. 5)

In children and teens, trauma can occur when they feel afraid, unsafe, helpless, or in danger. This can occur when they witness violence, illness, homelessness, abandonment, or other similar circumstance (Steele & Malchiodi, 2012).

Many scholars categorize trauma as either simple or complex. Simple trauma is a result of a single incident such as a natural disaster, car accident, an episode of violence or abuse, or witnessing an event that is extremely unordinary (Ford & Courtois, 2013). Complex trauma is when experiences of trauma are repetitive such as ongoing abuse, neglect, or violence. Complex traumas are almost always interpersonal traumas that occur because of a person's intentional acts or failure to act on behalf of another person (Ford & Courtois, 2013).

The Center for Disease Control and Prevention and Kaiser Study of Adverse Childhood Experiences (Felitti et al., 1998) is considered one of the largest studies to examine the prevalence of trauma in childhood – it included 17,337 participants. This study specifically examined adverse childhood experiences (ACEs). These include the experience of emotional, physical, sexual abuse; household challenges such as witnessing your mother treated violently, substance abuse or mental illness in the household, and being separated from a family member through divorce or incarceration; and emotional or physical neglect.

This study found that more than 60% of those in the study reported at least one ACE and more than 20% reported three or more ACEs. Additional research using this study and others replicating it have found that as the number of childhood experiences increases the risk for depression and anxiety increases, as does the risk for cancer, diabetes, and early death (Felitti et al., 1998).

Trauma and the Genetic System

Part of the reason for the negative outcomes associated with trauma is how it affects the genetic system. As discussed in Chapter 2, Andie Kealohi Sato Conching and Zaneta Thayer (2019) have proposed two models of how trauma alters the genetic system – an individual model and an intergenerational model. Mounting evidence has supported their assertions. Their individual model hypothesizes that the experience of trauma alters the epigenome resulting in modifying the expression of genes. In their summary of the research on trauma and epigenetic changes, Laura Ramo-Fernádez and her colleagues argued that the evidence points to how trauma changes the genes in the hypothalamus-pituitary-adrenal axis and the immune system. Drawing on research from various scholars, they write:

> PTSD-related health problems might stem from alterations in immune function, which might be partly mediated by epigenetic

changes. A comparison of whole blood DNA methylation in more than 14,000 genes between PTSD cases and healthy controls showed epigenetic changes of immune activation in PTSD patients, as some genes regulating the innate and adaptive immune systems were significantly less methylated. Methylation signatures of immune activation mechanisms were also found the in the peripheral blood cells investigated in an African American population with a PTSD diagnosis compared with health controls.

(Ramo-Fernández et al., 2015, pp. 707–708)

They point out that there isn't sufficient evidence to suggest a causal relationship between trauma and epigenetic changes, but the evidence is growing. Given the differences in immune functioning in those who have PTSD and those without at least part of this difference is likely attributed to epigenetic changes.

These changes have also been observed intergenerationally. As Conching and Thayer's (2019) intergenerational model suggests, parental stress can affect offspring's epigenome. In 2018, Ali Jawaid, Martin Roszkowski, and Isabelle Mansuy reviewed multiple articles examining the intergenerational epigenetic changes in animals and humans. They noted that the evidence is more robust in animals, but that the evidence for intergenerational epigenetic changes in humans is growing:

> Literature about the inheritance of the effects of traumatic stress in humans has slowly accumulated in the past decade. However, it remains thin and studies in humans generally lack clear "cause and effect" associations. . . . A recent study in Germany showed that low maternal bonding in mother and high levels of parental stress are associated with a clinical diagnosis of borderline personality disorder. . . . More recently, trauma exposure in holocaust survivors was shown to induce neuropsychiatric changes in their children and be associated with alterations in some epigenetic marks. . . . Although less studied from a mechanistic point of view, inter- and possible transgenerational inheritance of the effects of traumatic stress is supported empirical evidence in humans.
>
> (pp. 17–18)

Jawaid and his colleagues also argue that intergenerational epigenetic transmission might also be evolutionarily beneficial. They argue:

> With respect to the effects of traumatic stress, one can question whether their transmission has any evolutionary benefit, since many of these effects are negative. However, these effects may help the offspring better cope in certain conditions. . . . Most effects are

maladaptive in normal and insult-free condition suggesting that this could provide a way of "epigenetic natural selection" in which selection is driven by an organism's ability to adapt to a changing environment rather than survive the environmental adversity based on innate abilities.

(pp. 21–22)

They note that to support this assertion, additional studies that examine how humans and other animals cope with trauma and both adverse and not adverse conditions are necessary.

Trauma and the Individual System

Trauma that affects the expression of genes by changing the epigenome results in individual and intergenerational changes to the brain and body. This hypothesis is reflected in Bessel van der Kolk's seminal book, *The Body Keeps the Score*. In this book, van der Kolk argues that trauma results in the reorganization of the way the brain and body work. He writes:

> Being traumatized means continuing to organize your life as if the trauma were still going on – unchanged and immutable – as every new encounter or event is contaminated by the past. After trauma, the world is experienced with a different nervous system. The survivor's energy now becomes focused on suppressing inner chaos, at the expense of spontaneous involvement in their life.
>
> (p. 53)

Much research supports this van der Kolk's claim. In 2019, Meichen Yu and his colleagues examined the brains of 189 individuals with major depressive disorder and the brains of 39 without it. They found that those with depression had different brain connectivity compared to those without it. They also found that those with major depressive disorder who had also experienced childhood trauma had different brain connectivity than those who hadn't. They suggested that even though this study was done many years after these people had experienced childhood trauma, "the scar of prior trauma was evidence in functional dysconnectivity . . . childhood trauma-related network connectivity abnormalities were preserved and detected well into adulthood (pp. 8583, 8587–8588). In other words, those who had survived childhood trauma may have a different brain connectivity and symptom profiles of depression.

The changes in the brain and body can result in difficulty in emotional regulation. As Kerry Fraser, Diane MacKenzie, and Joan Versnel (2017) point out in their review of the research addressing treatment for children and teens who have experienced trauma:

> Children who have experienced complex trauma may have difficulty managing their emotion and arousal levels. A person's ability to manage states of emotional arousal without having an impact on other areas of functioning is dependent on staying regulated. . . . If a child has been neglected or is in a state of fear of high or low arousal for periods of time, the child misses the necessary sensory input required to make sense of the environment. If the child is not receiving sensory cues or input, everyday situations may be misinterpreted, potentially resulting in aggression, shutting down if overwhelmed, or running away.
> (p. 200)

The changes in the brain and body, resulting from trauma, can make sensory experiences seem overwhelming. There is not only evidence to support this in children but in adults as well (Ehring & Quack, 2010).

In *The Body Keeps the Score*, van der Kolk also draws on the research of Stephen Porges that I discussed in Chapter 2. Van der Kolk discusses how the social engagement system is activated when we experience trauma:

> The autonomic nervous system regulates three fundamental physiological states. The level of safety determines which one of these is activated at any particular time. Whenever we feel threated, we instinctively turn to the first level, social engagement. We call out for help, support, and comfort from the people around us. But if no one comes to our aid, or we're in immediate danger, the organism revert to a more primitive way to survive: *fight or flight*. We fight off our attacker, or we run to a safe place. However, I this fails . . . the organism tries to preserve itself by shutting down and expending as little energy as possible. We are then in a state of *freeze* or *collapse*. . . . [People who have experienced trauma] feel safe as long as they can limit their social contact to superficial conversations, but actual physical contact can trigger intense reaction.
> (pp. 80, 85)

As van der Kolk describes, trauma can make it extremely difficult to engage and create meaningful connections – making trauma a central focus of the attachment system.

Trauma and the Attachment System

As discussed in Chapter 3, the attachment system has certain steps that have been observed by Ed Tronkick and his colleagues in the Still-Face experiment. We reach out and invite connection; if our reaching isn't responded to, we protest or push trying to get connection or we turn away and shut down. If we still don't get the connection we seek, we go into meltdown. It's easy to see how this process overlaps with the process described by Porges and van der Kolk in response to trauma – reaching for help, shifting to fight or flight, and then going into freeze or collapse. In addition, trauma could exacerbate the basic moves of the attachment system.

Though trauma frequently occurs outside of the attachment system and has a large impact on it, I want to focus this discussion on trauma that occurs within the attachment system. Sue Johnson refers to this type of trauma as an attachment injury. In 2001, she and her colleagues Judy Makinen and John Millikin described attachment injuries as:

> [A] specific type of betrayal that is experienced in couple relationship. It is characterized as abandonment or a violation of trust. It is not a generally trust issue; it concerns a specific incident in which one partner is inaccessible and unresponsive in the face of the other partner's urgent need for the kind of support and caring we expect of attachment figures. . . . These events, if unresolved, not only damage the nature of the attachment bond between partners, they prevent the repair of this bond.
>
> (p. 149)

Though Johnson is focusing on couples, attachment injuries can occur in any attachment system. Research has shown that when children reach for a parent and the parent is unresponsive, this can result in problematic functioning (e.g., Spinazzola, van der Kolk, & Ford, 2018).

Johnson also distinguishes between ordinary highs and lows of ongoing relationships and attachment injuries. She argues that:

> Betrayals, such as attachment injuries, call into question basic beliefs about relationships, the other, and the self. As partners commit to an intimate relationship, they have an internal model of what the relationship will look like and how they expect to be treated. . . . When a partner cries out for help and there is no response, the sense of basic trust that is the "bedrock upon which the welfare of their bond depends" is shattered. The most basic assumption of attachment relationships, that one's partner will be there when he or she I needed, is suddenly destroyed. This shattering of basic assumptions is, in and of itself, disorienting, and it is part of the sense of helplessness that is perhaps the most salient feature of traumatic experience.
>
> (p. 150)

When we form attachment systems, these often come with expectations of safety and responsiveness. Though no one individual will always be responsive in the way we need at the exact moment we need it, we have emotional and cultural expectation placed on certain individuals. When these people betray our trust in specific time and in specific ways, we experience trauma.

Trauma and Triangulation

Trauma can also impact the triangulation system. As discussed earlier, trauma can result in poor emotional regulation and problematic reactivity. The triangulation system often serves as the system that can bind or suppress traumatic stress – often with damaging results (Kerr & Bowen, 1988). In a triangle, shame, guilt, and the stress that often accompanies a traumatic experience in some cases get passed down generationally through the triangulation system. Often, the triangle is maintained across generations through secrecy.

In 2019, Ashley Barnwell described how triangles of trauma that are maintained by secrecy can be passed intergenerationally. Drawing on the concept of "slow violence (Nixon, 2011)" – the idea that when trauma or violence is often ignored or downplayed it results in sustained injury across time, she argues that secrecy in the family can inflict trauma across generations. She writes:

> [I]n the context of family secrets, a double form of violence operates. With inherited secrets particularly, the cogs of relational and social obligation grind down the voices of the very people the secrets work against: the family itself. Families are compelled to edit their public face in response to judgement and sanction; and then new generations inherit these stigmas and maintain silence even when the direct threat may no longer exist.
>
> (p. 1116)

In recounting experiences of interviews conducted regarding family secrets, Barnwell describes how a family secret-shaped triangles across generations:

> Myrtle (73) describes how the pressure to present a "happy family" in everyday exchanges made her lonely and unwell. As a child, Myrtle was made to keep her mother's romantic relationship with her brother-in-law secret from the family. For fear Myrtle may disclose the relationship, the mother kept her separate from extended relatives. Years later, Myrtle discovered that relatives, reaching out, were also kept from her.
>
> (p. 1123)

Based on these and other experiences she documents, Barnard concludes:

> Secrets . . . operate as a form of social censorship that can play out slowly over lifetimes, affecting both specific families and stoking wider social ideas and values about what kinds of family lives and experiences are worthy or acceptable. . . . Acts of strategic silence, blindness and exclusion can happen quietly and slowly, as family respond to perceived social risk and sanctions. A close look at family secrets demonstrates how . . . events and social processes can wage an impact over time, wielding social power from within family and across generations.
>
> (p. 1124)

These arguments were supported by work Mira Helimaki and her colleagues conducted in 2020. Using the multi-actor dialogical methods for investigations of change happenings framework (Seikkula, Laitila, & Rober, 2012), these researchers examined video clips of therapy that was conducted with a family of four – two parents and a 9-year-old son, Mark, and an 8-year-old daughter, Clara. Through their analysis of the video clips in therapy, the researchers argued that a child's symptoms can act as a cover story to avoid talking about secrets occurring within the family. In the case of this family, the presenting issue was the son's oppositional behavior. However, during the fourth session of family therapy, it was discovered that the children's uncle had died by suicide. Helimaki and her colleagues write about the secrecy triangles that they observed in the family:

> Mark's symptomatic behavior, manifested in his speech about committing suicide, offered the opportunity for forbidden themes to be discussed. At the same time, however, he paradoxically kept the attention on himself, thereby implicitly protecting the sensitive topics from becoming a therapeutically relevant topic of discussion. Mark's threats to kill himself kept the suicide secret present, while simultaneously his provocative behavior, his infantile protest, kept the focus on him instead of on the secret. . . [the family's] secretive communication style produce a tense and psychologically distance climate, producing voices of ambivalence, hesitation, and confusion.
>
> (pp. 22–23)

The family was able to avoid the secrets by creating a triangle. The triangulation system kept the focus on the son and his "acting out," allowing the parents to ignore the pain that the mother was experiencing from her brother's death and for the father to be at times physically absent from therapy and often emotionally absent from the family.

Trauma and the Family System

Secrecy, disconnection in the attachment system, physiological changes, and emotional reactivity that can come about from trauma impact how the processes of threat-response, belonging, and individuality occur in the family system. They can also impact a family's ability to adapt. In Chapter 3, Olson's Circumplex Model was used to show how family balances cohesion and change, or, how families maintain autonomy and adapt. Olson argued that "the Circumplex Model is dynamic . . . changes can occur gradually over months or more rapidly. . . . These change often occur without specific planning." One of the ways in which gradual and rapid changes can occur is through trauma.

Families often adapt their togetherness and individuality processes to adapt to the added threat-response brought on by trauma. Sometimes these adaptations can help ameliorate traumatic stress and other times these adaptations can exacerbate traumatic stress (Singh, Lundy, Vidal de Haymes, & Caridad, 2011). If in response to trauma, if family increases it cohesion by giving more importance to the belonging processes, they may be able to help those affected by trauma lessen their physical and emotional reactivity (Sippel, Pietrzak, Charney, Mayes, & Southwick, 2015). Or if in a response to an injury in the attachment system, partners can effectively repair their connection, they may be able to use that connection to better adapt to the stress the attachment injury caused.

However, if in response to trauma a family system responds by trying to keep the trauma secret by creating a triangle to focus the attention elsewhere; or if the family alienates the person who has experienced trauma because of the system's inability to deal with the physiological and emotion changes that occur; or if an attachment injury occurs between partners and they are unable to repair; it is likely that the stress from the traumatic experience may threaten the autonomy of the family.

Trauma stresses the autonomy-generating processes in each system that creates the family system. When a person or relationship within a family system is traumatized, threat-responses are kicked into high gear – at a basic level trauma activates the FEAR emotional system, and the bodies fight, flight, or freeze responses. These responses may be centered around losing one's life, losing a relationship, or losing one's individuality. This leads to added pressure on the belonging and individuality processes – trauma makes it hard to form and maintain connections, and when it is not safe it's hard to pursue our own goals. When all of these processes are stressed, adaptation can be difficult or dysfunctional.

Trauma can lead to the family system no longer existing in its previous form – whether through death, divorce, or other relationships dissolution. The stress from trauma may result in irreversible changes that lead the family to be less adaptive to its environment. The family, because of trauma, may adjust the intensity of the response, but in a way that leads to its demise. Incidents of trauma are associated with poorer mental health creating potential risk of suicide ideation and attempts (Afifi et al., 2008). Traumatic experiences such as attachment injuries experiences can increase the risk of marital conflict and divorce (Warach & Josephs, 2019).

When family therapists are working with families in therapy, understanding how traumatic stress impacts each system of the family system is essential. By knowing how the threat-response, belonging, and individuality processes are stressed during trauma and how the family's capacity to adapt may be exceeded due to trauma is key to apply family therapy models and providing effective treatment. Knowing the resources that exist within the family and how attachment and triangulation systems can be used to mitigate the physiological and emotional effects on trauma is necessary to promote healing.

Trauma and the Sociocultural System

Traumatic stress doesn't just occur because of interactions with family members or within the family system. The family's environment, the sociocultural system, can and often is the source of trauma in a family system. What's more, the resources available to a family to cope with traumatic stress are often dependent on whether or not they hold privileged identities within their sociocultural system. Often, those who do not hold privilege identities can be retraumatized when they seek support for services in their communities. Much evidence has been accumulated to show how oppression that occurs in the sociocultural system can inflict trauma and can retraumatize families who seek help.

If you recall in Chapter 4, Iris Young outlined what she saw as the five faces of oppression. These include exploitation, marginalization, powerlessness, cultural imperialism, and violence. Looking at that list, you can see how the result of oppression is often trauma. Those who because of their identities in a given sociocultural system are oppressed, can experience historical and mass trauma.

In the 1990s the construct of historical trauma was developed to help contextualize the health disparities that are often experienced by marginalized groups. One example where researchers examined historical trauma was in the lives of the Indigenous people of North America. In their 2019 systematic review on historical trauma among Indigenous populations in the United States and Canada, Joseph Gone and his colleagues outlined how European colonizers, through violence, cultural imperialism, and other forms of oppression created what is called "historical trauma" seen in many Indigenous communities today. They wrote:

> The Indigenous peoples of North American lived and interacted through the continent irrespective of current national boundaries.

> Such boundaries came into existence through processes of European colonization and settlement, often arbitrarily dividing self-designated communities and mutually recognized kin. The polices of these nation-state subsequently shaped Indigenous lives and experiences in profound ways. . . . Indigenous historical trauma is universally characterized as originating in the brutal process of colonization (e.g., conquest, plunder, impoverishment), which resulted in population decline and subsequent subjugation of Indigenous people. . . . Indigenous historical trauma differs from ordinary lifetime psychological trauma in key ways: it is *colonial* in origin, *collective* in impact, *cumulative* across adverse events, and (especially) *cross-generational* in transmission of risk and vulnerability.
>
> (p. 21)

Gone and colleagues conducted their systematic review to provide a synthesis of the evidence that is available regarding Indigenous historical trauma and its impacts. Specifically, they wanted to answer the question, "What do we know empirically about the health impact of Indigenous historical trauma among Indigenous populations in the United States and Canada?" After reviewing 32 studies, they concluded that there wasn't sufficient evidence to answer that question definitively. However, their review highlighted many studies that showed a significant association between historical loss and symptoms indicative of trauma – depression, anxiety, higher rates of substance use, and/or suicidal ideation.

Trauma inflicted through oppression in the sociocultural system isn't just confined to historical issues. Though it often has historical roots, race-based trauma is trauma that occurs in the sociocultural system but that affects every system that creates the family system. In 2020, Robert Carter, Katherine Kirkinis, and Veronica Johnson examined the association between race-based trauma and trauma symptoms that are associated with post-traumatic stress disorder. Using a sample of 421 adults, they had individuals write down memorable events of racism or racial discrimination that they had experienced and had them indicate how they felt after the event. They also asked them to complete a checklist of 40 trauma symptoms. When they examined the association between these two measures, they noted:

> The results of this study indicate that negative, race-based encounters seem to produce PTSD-like symptoms/injuries – particularly dissociation, anxiety, depression, the mixed array of symptoms associated with trauma history, sleep disturbance, and sexual problems. That is, it seems that experiences other than exposure or being a witness to violent or accidental death/threatened death, actual/threatened serious injury, or actual/threatened sexual violence can produce trauma symptomology.
>
> (p. 16)

Based on these finds, they further argued:

> The current definition of trauma in the DSM-5 may be problematic, in that it limits the ability for people with other types of trauma to access appropriate diagnoses, medical care, and insurance reimbursement. A modification to the DSM-5 criteria of PTSD to allow for a wider array of experiences, along with a deeper understanding of reactions of people exposed to race-based stress or trauma can be helpful for mental health clinicians and may guard against the common pathologizing misdiagnoses, particularly for Black clients.
>
> (p. 16)

Carter and colleagues are pointing to the notion that often families look for help within the community to deal with traumatic stress; however, frequently these interactions can result in worsening traumatic stress or re-traumatization.

Evidence for this was found by Petrea Taylor in 2020. In her study, Taylor examined the experience of 32 women who had left an abusive partner and sought help for suicidality. After conducting the interview with the women, Taylor found that many women in this situation experienced what she called "system entrapment" – being dehumanized by the invalidation of a health-care provider when seeking help. Taylor writes:

> The basic psycho-social problem for women's help-seeking, *Systemic Entrapment*, involves feeling controlled and minimized as a result of perceiving a health care provider's invalidation or lack of empathy. The *System* represents the health care system and *Entrapment* represents a feeling of being trapped and dehumanized. While *System Entrapment* is the central problem, two other forms of *Entrapment* influence women's difficulty in seeking help . . . *Abuser Entrapment* represent feeling hopeless about escaping intimate partner violence . . . [and it] illustrates a novel concept of dehumanization in relation to being abused leading to a loss of meaning in life and a disconnection from living . . . *Trauma Entrapment* represent the despair and hopelessness of suicidality, leaving litter energy to escape psychological pain.
>
> (pp. 534–535)

In other words, when a person with an often-oppressed identity, (in this case a women) experiences trauma (in this case intimate partner violence), this can result in traumatic stress (in this case suicidality). However, because of the dehumanization this person can further experience trauma when they seek help in their sociocultural system. When they interact with those in power (in this case a health-care provider) they are marginalized, invalidated, and rendered powerless. This can exacerbate traumatic stress and deter the person from seeking help in the future.

When a person or a family system seeks help in the sociocultural system for traumatic stress and the bids for helps are met with dehumanization and marginalization, this serves not only to exacerbate their stress but the capacity for the family system to maintain autonomy and to adapt. When family systems experience trauma and then are re-traumatized through help seeking, it can result in the breakdown of relationships and connection and result in changes to the family system that cannot be reversed.

Chapter Recap

More so than attachment theory or the postmodern critique, family systems theory can conceptualize contextual clinical issues and how they affect the family system. One example of this is trauma. Trauma can take many forms – simple or complex, historical or current, but trauma affects every system that creates the family system. Trauma can change our genes and the expression of our genes through our epigenome – resulting in intergenerational changes. When trauma occurs our brain and bodies can also change – our fight, flight, and social engagement systems can be on high alert, leading us to being on edge and find difficulty engaging socially.

Trauma can occur in and affects the attachment system. When trauma occurs in the attachment system, it is known as an attachment injury. Attachment injuries can affect the autonomy of attachment system – couples who experience attachment injury are at greater risk of divorce. When trauma occurs, often a triangulation system based on secrecy will form. Sometimes, this will result in someone in the triangle having symptoms of problems that distract from and protect the secret. When the family system or one of its members experiences trauma, the family can adapt by activating or emphasizing specific autonomy processes. Evidence suggest that families who strengthen their belongingness ties can often respond better to traumatic stress. However, if there is alienation through the activation of individuality processes at the expense of belonging or if the family shuts down when so much stress is present, the family may lose its autonomy.

Trauma also occurs in the sociocultural system. Historical and race-based trauma are just two ways that those with power oppress other, resulting in traumatic stress. What's more when those with marginalized identities seek help, they can be further traumatized. Often those in power will treat those with traumatic stress in ways that serve to dehumanize their experience and put even greater stress on that individual and their family system.

Questions to Consider

1. Do you think that family systems theory provides a better explanation for trauma than attachment theory or the postmodern critique? Why or why not?
2. What other theories could potentially be useful for understanding how trauma affects the family system?
3. Where does family systems theory fall short in explaining trauma? What new evidence would we need about family systems theory to better predict and explain the effects of trauma on families?
4. What are other ways that the sociocultural system can inflict trauma and retraumatize families? What role do family therapists play in continuing this pattern? How could we make it better?

Chapter 11

Family Systems Theory and Family Therapy Models

If you picked up this book to learn how to do family therapy, you're probably frustrated at this point. And unfortunately, I'm not going to ease your frustration in this chapter. Though family systems theory is used to develop models of family therapy, it isn't a psychotherapy model. Family systems theory doesn't make predictions about which interventions will work best with families or how many sessions a family will need to reach its goal. It doesn't tell us how to ask the right question, when to do an enactment, or which members of the family should join for therapy. Family systems theory doesn't have hypotheses about what makes for good therapy or a good therapist. But I do think family systems theory can help improve family therapy models.

In the preceding chapters, I've outlined what I see as the evidence for family systems theory, and I've also highlighted some of the limitations and weaknesses of the theory. And I've tried to be transparent about the fact that with new evidence family systems theory may need to be amended or discarded for another theory. In other words, I feel like I have addressed many of the issues that make for good theory, and I feel that I have made a case as to why psychotherapy models can build solidly on family systems theory. However, does that mean that we need to throw out the models we do have and start over? Do we need to develop new models from scratch?

I don't think so. Many of the ideas and arguments I've presented here have been discussed for decades. Salvador Minuchin wrote about them:

> Family structure is the invisible set of functional demands that organizes the ways in which family members interact. A family is a system that operates through transactional patterns. Repeated transactions establish patterns of how, when, and to whom we relate, and these patterns underpin the system... Transactional patterns regulate family member's behavior.... Thus the system maintains itself. If offers resistance to change beyond a certain range, and maintains preferred patterns as long as possible.... But the family structure must be

able to adapt when circumstances change. The continued existence of the family as a system depends on a sufficient range of patterns, the availability of alternative transactional patterns, and the flexibility to mobilize them when necessary. Since the family must respond to internal and external changes, it must be able to transform itself in ways that meet new circumstances without losing the continuity that provides a frame of reference for its members.

(pp. 39–40)

Minuchin further argued:

> The family is an open system in transformations; that is, it constantly receives and sends inputs to and from the extrafamilial, and it adapts to the different demands of the developmental stages it faces. . . . A family is subject to inner pressure coming from developmental changes in its own family members and subsystems and to outer pressure coming from demands to accommodate to the significant social institutions that have an impact on the family members. Responding to these demands from both within and without requires a constant transformation of the position of family members in relation to one another, so they can grow while the family system maintains continuity.
>
> (p. 50)

Kerr and Bowen (1988) make similar claims. In their work, they use the concept of differentiation of self to discuss adaptation to families. They argue that differentiation of self is the concept that determines why certain families are better suited to specific environment than others.

> Family systems theory uses the concept of differentiation of self, an aspect of which is adaptiveness to stress. Families with a low level of differentiation are not inferior families. They are less adaptive families.
>
> (p. 246)

Further Kerr and Bowen write:

> As differentiation and adaptiveness decrease, family systems theory predicts that the incidence and severity of life problems will increase . . . Depending on the number and type of events an individual or family must adapt to, anxiety may increase or decrease accordingly . . . The less adaptive an individual or family to stress, the more likely that potentially stressful events encountered earlier in life will exceed that individuals of families ability to adapt.
>
> (p. 235)

They are echoing the adaptations discussed in Chapter 6. If the family is an adaptable system, then some families are likely to be better suited to the environment then they are in than others. And, as an adaptable system, the family senses stimuli in their environment and try to adapt based on the intensity of the stimuli.

Family systems theory as presented in this book is similar to ideas that have been discussed for decades. These ideas have been the foundation for many of the approaches that family therapists learn and practice. The models that have been developed, taught, and practiced for years build on a strong theoretical base.

So, I don't think we need to throw out the models we have, but I do think we can make them better. Though the ideas proposed by Bowen, Minuchin, and others are like those discussed in this book, there are many things that have come about since they proposed their models. We know more about genes, epigenetics, the human brain and body, attachment, triangles, and about the sociocultural system. To make these models better, and to incorporate the new evidence we have gained, we need to shift the debate family therapists and researchers are having about psychotherapy models. For decades now, family therapists have been engaged in a "common factors versus model-driven" psychotherapy debate.

Family Systems Theory and the Great Psychotherapy Debate

As I described in Chapter 1, multiple studies showed that when you compared models of family therapy, there isn't much difference between them. In 1993, Shadish and his colleagues conducted a meta-analysis of 163 randomized clinical trials and found that there were no significant differences between models and no significant differences between couple and family therapy models and individual models. In the 2004 Cannabis Youth Treatment Study, Diamond and colleagues (2006) recruited 600 adolescents and randomly assigned them to either individual therapy, family education and individual therapy, a community reinforcement approach, or to family therapy. These researchers also found no differences between the approaches on cannabis use.

These and other studies (Sprenkle, Davis, & Lebow, 2013) have led many family therapists and researchers to accept what is known as the "dodo verdict." This idea comes from Lewis Carrols's *Alice in Wonderland*. In *Alice in Wonderland*, many characters in the book become wet. To get them dry, the dodo bird issues a challenge – everyone must run around until they are dry. After all the characters ran, they came to the dodo bird and asked who had won. The dodo bird responded, "Everybody has won, and all must have prizes." In

1936, Saul Rosenzweig applied this idea to psychotherapy, suggesting that one model of psychotherapy wasn't better than any other, and therefore all of them could have prizes. More than ten years before the writing of this book, Jaqueline Sparks and Barry Duncan (2010) concluded that "the preponderance of the evidence suggests the dodo verdict to be true to form in marriage and family therapy" (p. 361). Like induvial therapy, they argue, there isn't one family therapy model that is better than another.

This has led many to argue for what is called "common factors" of family therapy. The common factors approach asserts that there are specific things that account for change in therapy that are not model dependent. These include extratherapeutic factors – the client's job or developmental life events; the therapeutic alliance – the quality of the relationship between therapist and client; and, hope – the expectation that going to therapy will result in positive change (Duncan, Miller, Wampold, & Hubble, 2010). Though those who advocate for a common factors approach do see value in models, they see models as the conduit for enacting common factors (Sprenkle, Davis, & Lebow, 2013).

If one model isn't better than another, then can we make our model better? Or is this just a useless endeavor? Many do see value in developing and refining models to improve family therapy practice. In her 2019 book *Attachment Theory in Practice*, Sue Johnson argued against a common factors approach. She acknowledges the "dodo verdict" but pushes back on it, noting that:

> The large justification for this orientation [common factors of change] is that all treatments in large outcome studies are seem to be equally effective, so specific models and interventions are interchangeable. In fact, this generalization is unfounded and is based on placing many different studies of varying quality into a soup called meta-analysis and coming up results that are often meaningless. . . . Perhaps the most considered variables in the study of general change factors seems to be the quality of the alliance with the therapist and client engagement in the therapy process. This promise is that, if we get these general factors right, then suddenly the task of therapy, to create change, will become simple and manageable.
> (pp. 3–4)

Though I would disagree with the assertion that results of meta-analytic studies are often meaningless, I do agree that the results have often been overgeneralized – we don't often know what works for whom, when it works, or how it works. Johnson also notes that common factors of change often only account for a small variance of change and that these common factors are often poorly defined.

A similar argument was by Thomas Sexton and his colleagues in 2004. They argued that:

> Despite the contributions of the common factors perspective, it does not explain the complexity of change or the process through which change takes place. In their current form, common factors are presented as discrete factors that . . . are neither operationally defined, contextualized within the clinical process into which they might fit, or explicated as to the mechanisms that might promote their outcome. In fact, many of the factors that find their way to common factors lists are actually the outcomes of an undefined relational and interpersonal process rather than the therapeutic change mechanism they imply.
>
> (p. 138)

If you can't tell by now, I'm partial to the Johnson and Sexton arguments. But I think we need a shift in the way we have this debate. Instead of getting stuck in the common factor vs. model evaluation debate, we need to spend more time developing and evaluating theory. Adding theory to this debate opens new possibilities.

Theory and Models

In Chapters 8 and 9, I made an argument as to why I see family systems theory as a superior theory to build a practice. When comparing it to both the postmodern critique and attachment theory, I argued that family systems theory was able to be falsified (and therefore has an advantage over postmodernism) and better accounts for relationship complexity (and therefore has advantages over attachment theory). To me, this is the important debate.

Family therapy models are only as good as the theories they are built upon. I would argue that one reason that many have argued for the "dodo bird verdict" is that (especially when it comes to family therapy) our theories have remained stagnate. This argument was echoed by Karen Wampler and her colleagues in 2019:

> One of the challenges that we face as a field is that we are largely still beholden to the founding theorists who were instrumental in our fields development (e.g., Minuchin, Bowen, Satir). There has not been enough innovation in terms of new theory development or research-based validation of foundational theories in the last 50 years. . . . In the decades to come, a new wave of innovation in the development of . . . theories must occur.
>
> (p. 11)

Stephen Fife has made a similar argument. In 2020, he wrote a chapter for the *Handbook of Systemic Family Therapy* called "Theory: The Heart of Systemic Family Therapy." In it, he argues that good family therapy practice is theory driven. He lays out what he argues is the role of theory including describing, explaining, and predicting family interactions. He chronicles the work of von Bertalanffy and others in the development of family systems theory, but notes this theory has become diluted. He writes:

> In spite of its rich history and tradition, the field of family therapy has struggled to maintain the same theoretical richness and evolution as its dynamic beginning. The theoretical momentum of [family therapy's] early period and the resurgence of theoretical energy brought by postmodernism and feminist scholars have waned.
>
> (p. 298)

Fife also suggests that currently many training programs and therapists avoid theory, instead focusing their time on models, not realizing the theory a model is built upon may be flawed.

He further argues that:

> Systemic therapists and scholars clearly recognize the benefit of rigorous scientific methods. Yet the field may not appreciate the importance of rigorous theorizing to enhance the conceptual, empirical, and clinical strength and health of the discipline. In order to maintain a vibrant and influential discipline, we must continue to improve upon current theories and develop new ones. . . . Theory development in [family therapy] began with careful thinking about prevailing views of human beings and relationships, recognizing their limitations, and exploring alternative ideas. It also involved discussion, debate, and critique of the predominate ideas and theories. . . . Future theoretical development in our field will likely follow a similar path.
>
> (p. 310)

To me, the argument that Wampler and Fife are making is like some of the couples I see in therapy. Some couples come to therapy and describe their relationship as being "more like roommates." They live together, they complete tasks together, they co-parent together, they don't really fight, but they come to therapy because their relationship isn't fulfilling. The partnership doesn't challenge them. There is no conflict, so there is no growth.

In some ways, the field of family therapy is in the same rut. We've settled into a practice that works well, and for the most part, gets the job done. But its theories aren't growing, aren't in conflict, and aren't being challenged. At the same time, we've had an unprecedented growth in the empirical understanding of family relationships, how the family is affected by genes and epigenetics, and the essential role the sociocultural systems play in family relationships. And I think we can use this new knowledge to make our models better.

The Way Forward

Some are already doing this. If you recall in Chapter 4, I alluded to the work of Teresa McDowell, Carmen Kunduson-Martin, and Maria Bermudez. In 2018, they published a book called *Sociocultural Attuned Family Therapy*. In it, they argue that the models of family therapy have looked much beyond the border of the family system. If we want our clients and their families to be healthy and thriving, we must use family therapy to create what they called third-order change – "third order change is a shift in the relationship to sociocultural systems that expands possibilities and enables transformation of one's life" (p. 22).

To make this change, they draw on research that has shown the effect power, privilege, and oppression can have on families and argue that family therapy models can be improved when family therapy do six things:

Attune – understand, resonate with, and responding to experience within societal contexts.
Name – identify what is unjust or has been overlooked – amplify silenced voices.
Value – acknowledge the worth of that which has been minimized or devalued.
Intervene – support relational equity – disrupt oppressive power dynamics.
Envision – provide space to imagine just relational alternative.
Transform – collaborate to make what is imagined real – third order change.

(p. 24)

Then McDowell, Knudson-Marin, and Bermudez take these principles and apply them to various family therapy models. They show how family therapy models can and must move beyond the border of the family and how adding these practices into therapy can do just that. To validate these claims, researchers will need to conduct trials comparing models with these practices and models without them. But their work is the first step in the process.

I believe that this is the best approach to building better models. Some model developers, like Mona Fishbane (2013), have taken neurobiology research and applied it to couples therapy, but I think there is value in examining how this research can enhance our understanding of triangles and other interactions between family member, not just couples. I also think model developers would be well served to think about how the research coming forward about genes and epigenetics can enhance and improve family therapy models. The more we use the evidence regarding the systems that create the family system, the better I think our models can become.

To improve family therapy models, family systems theory needs to be rigorously evaluated. The evidence that is produced through research needs to be applied to family systems theory so it can either be validated or changed – we can no longer afford to simply state a study is guided by family systems theory. We need to take the evidence and change or extend family systems theory (Chen et al., 2017). As this evidence is accumulated, model developers need to use this evidence to change or extend family therapy models. These changes need to be evaluated through research to see if outcomes improved. Then, this evidence could be applied not only to the model but also to family systems theory. This would create a reciprocal relationship between theory and research and between theory and models. Only when theory, research, and model development work together can we expect to see improvement in family therapy outcomes.

Chapter Recap

To improve family therapy treatment, many have argued that we need to focus on common factors of change. Those who support this path rely on research that suggests that no one family therapy model does better than any other model. However, there are others who argue that common factors of change are often poorly defined and represent relational and interpersonal processes rather than therapeutic change mechanisms. They suggest that model evaluation and comparison will eventually help us understand the change process in all its complexity.

Yet another way to improve models is by improving theory. The theories on which family therapy models are built haven't always been rigorously examined in the last decades. What's more, the field of family therapy will only stay vibrant when we have robust debates around family relationships and theories that explain them. As a field, we need to have a renewed focus on evaluating theory and using the evidence we get by testing hypotheses to change our models accordingly. This path is the most likely to result in improved practice.

Questions to Consider

1. Which stance do you find most compelling when it comes to improving family therapy models? Common factors? Model evaluation? Theory development?

2. In your reading, do you think that the evidence is enough to support one path for improving models over another?
3. How could you see each of these pathways working together? Are there points of overlap?
4. Do you think the field of family therapy needs a renewed focus on theory? Would our time and efforts be well spent improving theory?

Chapter 12

Conclusions and Recommendations

Of all the great experiences I had during graduate school, one that has stuck occurred every spring in my master's program in courses with Dr. Joseph Wetchler. During one class period, Joe would have us slide all the desks to the side of the room, have us stand up, and he would begin to read epistemological statements in pairs (these statements are taken from Piercy & Sprenkle, 1986). Pointing to one wall in the room, he would say, for example, "Historical information *is important* in understanding and changing present functioning." Then he would point to the opposite wall and say, "Historical information *is unimportant* in understanding and changing present functioning." As students, we would then have to pick between each wall to indicate how much we agreed with either statement. If we strongly agreed that "historical information was important" we would stand next to that wall; if we thought it was "unimportant," we would stand next to the opposite wall; if we thought it was somewhere in the middle, we would find a space somewhere near the middle of the classroom. Once each of us were situated, Joe would walk over to us and ask us to provide a rationale for the position we chose. We had to argue why we thought the location we had chosen best represents how families change, and how therapy works best. Sometimes our answers were well grounded; sometimes they were made up on the spot.

At Purdue Calumet, where I completed my master's degree, this game was known as "The Episte-Weenie" game. The rumor was that one time as Joe was completing the exercise, a student who had perpetually been in the middle on each epistemological pairing, walked right to the middle of the room and declared themselves the "Episte-Weenie" for failing to take a firm stance on anything. Whether this story of the name of this exercise is true or not, I think the exercise that Joe had us do highlights one of the main reasons I wrote this book. In Chapter 11, I quoted both Karen Wampler and her colleagues as well as Stephen Fife who argue that we need to have a rich debate around theory. This debate, unlike many of the answers I gave in the Epsite-Weenie game, needs to be grounded in science. If we are going to keep our field vibrant, we need, as Karen Wampler and colleagues wrote, "a new wave of innovation" in theory development to occur. In part, I see this book as an answer to that call.

Though many of the ideas presented here aren't necessarily new to family systems theory, I would argue that in some cases, the claims I am making stand at odds with some of the current thinking in the field. And I think that disagreement is important. I have talked in this book about the connection between research and theory – that both inform and help each other course correct; but when theory and research don't get debated, examined, and criticized, they become stagnant.

I hope this doesn't happen to what I've argued in this book. In fact, I would see it as a good step for family therapy if the claims I've presented were proven wrong by future research. This would show that as family therapists and researchers, we engaged in the hard work of moving the field forward.

Debating Family Systems Theory

So, if you'll indulge me, I've created my own list of statements that could be used in an "Epsite-Weenie" game. This list includes what I see as the chief arguments made in this book and the assumptions on which these arguments rest. Paired with these statements are claims and arguments made by other theories and researchers that aim to explain family interactions. My goal in pairing these statements is that you'll think critically about what I have presented here and that you will challenge my arguments when you think they have come up short. In other words, I hope you'll take this list to, as Stephen Fife said, think about the "prevailing views of human beings and relationships, recognize their limitations, and explore alternative ideas" (p. 310).

As you read the list, ask yourself: Do you agree with what has been presented here? Do you think that the evidence we have is sufficient to support the hypotheses that the family is an autonomous and adaptable system? Did you find yourself agreeing with the arguments and claims made in this book? Or did you find yourself drawn to other arguments? Did you think there are things on this list that are missing or an additional argument that could be made?

Here is the list:

| Family relationships are unique. The interactions that occur within the family are more important to well-being and health than interactions with people outside the family. | Humans are social creatures. It doesn't matter who we are interacting with, rather what matters is that we have interactions with others that promote well-being and health. |

Biological theories provide a foundation for understanding the human family and the interactions that occur within the family.	Biological theories can tell us little about current families. Given the unique cognitive and emotional abilities of humans, we need separate theories to describe family interactions.
Like all other organisms, the family is a biologically autonomous system. It has rule-based, boundary-making processes that generate and maintain the family.	All human systems are language- and meaning-generating systems. The reality and meaning we experience are interactional phenomena generated in conversation and action with ourselves and each other.
The family system has three main processes that make it an autonomous system – threat-response, belonging, and individuality. The processes are interdependent and no one process is more important than the other.	Belonging and connection are the foundation of the family system, and therefore, the most important process. Without a secure sense of connection, we feel unsafe to explore our individuality.
The family is an adaptable system. The family system responds to stress from inside and outside of the system by making changes to its rule-based, boundary-making processes. The goal of these adaptations is to help the family maintain autonomy.	The family system follows fixed developmental stages. Though there are cultural differences in these stages, these stages begin when a partnership is formed and end when one or both partners die.
Gene and epigenetics are important to the autonomy and adaptation processes in families. Genes interact with the other systems in the family to shape interactions.	Genes are assumed to be more significant to family interactions than they really are. Other factors play a larger role in family interactions than genes.
Our brains and bodies evolved to learn from and adapt to the social behavior of others. Social behavior we see in others can trigger physiological responses in our bodies that are often outside of our awareness.	Humans have complete control over their reactions and responses. When we engage with another person, we can choose how we will react.
Attachment relationships can be formed between any two people in a family. One attachment relationship is not necessarily more important than another.	Attachment relationships are formed primarily with caregivers and romantic partners. These relationships are more important than other dyadic relationships.
Triangles are a naturally occurring biological system that shapes family interactions across generations and throughout development.	Dyadic relationships are not influenced by a third person. The connection we have with one person is not influenced by the connections we have with others.

| The sociocultural system in which the family is embedded shapes all family interactions – you can't understand the family without knowing its environment. | Families can alter and shape their own interactions independent of influences in the environment. |

In the preceding chapters, I've tried to make a compelling argument that family systems theory is rooted in science. I'm hoping that as you went through this list, you thought that the evidence I presented throughout this book was compelling enough to have you support at least some of the claims of family systems theory. As I wrote in Chapter 1, my goal of this book was to outline the science linked to family systems theory. I wanted to give an overview of the research that has come about since the people like Virginia Satir, Murray Bowen, and Salvador Minuchin proposed their ideas. I wanted to present the evidence that supported the hypotheses that the family is an autonomous and adaptable system. I wanted to show that without a strong, scientifically supported theory to ground our practice, our practice risks becoming outdated.

But more than that, I hope that what I've written pushes you to bring your own voice, ideas, and understanding to the debate about family systems theory. I hope it sparks an interest evaluating the science of family systems theory and challenging its claims. I hope that in doing so, you take part in reigniting the "theoretical richness" that spurred family therapy in the beginning.

Two Suggestions

Don't know where to start? I have two suggestions.

We need to read better. Reading better requires us to return to the foundational text of theory and practice. Instead of reading textbooks that summarize a theory or model, we need to go to the source and engage the original ideas that the author presented. Though introductory texts have their place, I worry that we rely on them too heavily as the way to learn about theory and models. When ideas get summarized into introductory texts, they lose the richness and nuance that they originally had.

To read better we also need to read more widely. As I've noted, many fields of science have contributed to the understanding of the systems that create the family system. If we want to understand family relationships, we must read research for a variety of disciplines. Though I've summarized some of the research regarding genetics, evolution, the nervous system, emotions, attachment, triangulation, and power and privilege, there is so much more to learn. It isn't necessary for family therapists and scholars to become experts on all these topics, but if we want to engage in debates about theory, we need to be actively keeping up with the new evidence.

To be able to read much of the science that's out there, family therapists are going to need better statistical literacy. If you're like many of my graduate students, when you read a journal article, you sometimes read the introduction and then jump to the discussion and conclusion sections. In some cases, that may be okay. But if we really want to understand the research, we need to be able to decipher what was found and what it means.

I've tried to make it easier for you to read better. I've included an appendix in this book that cites and summarizes many of the research articles and texts that the hypotheses and arguments I make in this book. In addition, I've pulled together resources you can use to better understand research methods and statistics. I hope you'll read and examine the evidence I've used to support family systems theory, so can draw your own conclusions.

But just reading the research isn't enough. Not only has the science of human relationships advanced since the first research on family systems theory, but so has technology. Today, we have greater access to research and scientific finds than ever before. Whether it be through a podcast, YouTube, forums on social media, or other forms of engagement, there are endless options for family therapists to learn about research. These platforms are great for keeping up with current research that is applicable to our practice. What's more, it's also important for researchers to *create the content and add to* these platforms. Historically, researchers and therapists have been bad at communicating to people outside of their discipline about what they do and why it's important. While this is changing a bit, it's important for family therapy researchers to find ways to communicate the importance of our practice and the findings of our research.

This technology also lets us engage and debate in new ways. In addition to my job as a practicing therapist, I train future family therapists to do research. One of my favorite parts of this job is having us read a book or research article and come to class and discuss, break down, and debate what we read. Unfortunately, for most therapists, this type of discussion and debate ends after their formal graduate school training. Though there are requirements for continuing education, these presentations are often with larger groups and focused on how to do therapy rather than debating theory and research.

I think it is important for us as family therapists to use technology platforms to engage in similar debates that we had in graduate school settings. Platforms that allow for messaging, digital conferences, and other forms of communication would allow us to propose ideas and debate them. Instead of waiting for annual conferences, we could connect therapists and researchers together to critique the evidence and how we interpret it.

In the second appendix of this book, I've created a list of platforms that are useful for helping to find and engage with research. It is by no means an exhaustive list, but it does include podcasts, websites, and other content generating platforms that I relied on to find the evidence I summarized in this book.

By reading better and engaging differently, I hope that the field and practice of family therapy will grow. I hope that in the decades to come, the evidence base for family systems theory can be used to improve our models and help provide better care to more couples and more families. As we get better at what we do, my hope is the public will see the value that our practice brings, and that when families are struggling, they won't hesitate to seek out a family therapist.

That way when someone asks me what I do, I can say, "I'm a family therapist," and I'll have no need to lie.

Appendix A
Read Better

The following is a list of readings I think are essential to family systems theory. Though this isn't an exhaustive list, it contains books and articles that I think are a critical starting point. I have provided the citation, a brief description of the book, and then some details on why it is important and relevant for understanding family systems theory. I have broken down the readings to reflect the outline of this book. I have listed readings for biological systems, autonomy and adaptation; the genetic and individual system; the attachment, triangulation, and family systems; and for the sociocultural system. My goal in providing this list is to allow the reader to dive deeper into the claims made in this book and to examine the evidence for themselves.

Biological Systems, Autonomy, and Adaptation

The research around biological autonomy, adaptation, and systems has a long history. In this section, I've included readings from some of the early scholars of biological systems, articles that trace the history and books that show the current thinking about autonomy and adaptation.

von Bertalanffy, L. (1969). *General system theory: Foundations, development, applications.* New York: George Braziller.

Summary

This book is a compilation of writings of Ludwig von Bertalanffy. In this text, von Bertalanffy outlines the hypotheses of his systems theory and details evidence for each of these hypotheses. In addition, he outlines mathematical considerations of systems theory, proposes how systems theory could potentially unify science, and argues for all living things to be seen in as systems. He also applies system theory to psychology and psychiatry and argues how systems theory provides clear testable hypothesis for these disciplines.

Importance for family systems theory

I think any serious examination of family systems theory needs to start with von Bertalanffy's writings. Though, as I note in the book, some of his ideas and hypotheses have evolved through the years based on new evidence, many of his assumptions and proposals are still very relevant today. I especially recommend that family therapists read Chapters 6, 7, 8, and 9 of this book. These chapters contain the clear hypothesis and application and extension of these hypotheses to fields of study relevant to family therapy.

Rosslenbroich, B. (2014). *On the origin of autonomy: A new look at the major transitions in evolution* (Vol. 5). Berlin: Springer Science & Business Media.

Summary

On the Origin of Autonomy: A New Look at the Major Transitions in Evolution by Bernd Rosslenbroich (2014) provides an extensive overview of autonomy and adaptation and how it has shaped humans' (and other animals) brains, bodies, and behavior throughout evolution. In it he traces the concept of biological autonomy from von Bertalanffy to present-day thinking and provides a definition of it. Using this definition, he then outlines autonomy processes and how they resulted in major evolutionary transitions. He also discusses the evolution of the nervous system, the brain, and behavior and discusses special features of biological autonomy in humans. He finally proposes what he sees as questions left to be answered and discusses how research in other domains may help shed more light on biological autonomy.

Importance for family systems theory

I think that this book provides the clearest and most relevant definition of biological autonomy for family therapists. Though much of the discussion about macro-evolutionary trends may not be of interest to some family therapists, the discussion of the unique aspects of biological autonomy in humans and how autonomy played a role in the evolution of the nervous system and the brain and behavior are especially relevant to understanding family systems theory. If you don't want to read the whole book, I'd recommend reading Chapters 1, 3, 10, 11, 12 to glean the information most relevant for family systems theory.

Moreno, A., & Mossio, M. (2015). *Biological autonomy: A Philosophical and Theoretical Enquiry* (*History, philosophy, and theory of the life sciences*) (Vol. 12). New York: Springer Science & Business Media.

Summary

Biological Autonomy: A Philosophical and Theoretical Enquiry by Alvaro Moreno and Matteo Mossio (2015) focuses on biological autonomy and how it gives rise to interconnected systems. In it, Moreno and Mossio discuss cognition in organisms and how it is a product of the autonomy and adaptation. They discuss organisms and levels of autonomy, propose a hierarchical structure to autonomy, and argue that evolution of hierarchical levels of autonomy gave rise to cognition and social interactions. They also suggest that biological autonomy is grounded in thermodynamics.

Importance for family systems theory

This book is particularly important in supporting the argument of systems within systems. The systems that create the family system are hierarchical, not in the sense of their importance or relevance to the family system, but in their evolutionary order. This book discusses the science behind the evolution of the hierarchy and shows how social processes are the result.

Carr, A. (2015). The evolution of systems theory. In *Handbook of family therapy* (pp. 27–43). New York: Routledge.

Summary

The Evolution of Systems Theory by Alan Carr in *The Handbook of Family Therapy* (2016) provides a detailed description of the evolution of family systems theory and some of the major transitions that have occurred. In it he details general systems theory, cybernetics, and the work of Gregory Bateson. In addition, Carr outlines what he sees as the 20 propositions of systems theory applied to the practice of couple and family therapy. These include propositions regarding boundaries, patterns, stability and change, and complexity.

Importance for family systems theory

Carr's work provides a concise but informative view of family systems theory. I believe that this chapter also shows how family systems theory has lost focus. Carr delineates more than 20 propositions – most of which can be folded into the concepts of autonomy and adaptation. However, it also provides a strong argument for his proposals and understanding these proposals can help better critique the proposals of family systems theory constituted in this book.

The Genetic and Individual Systems

Genes, epigenetics, the nervous system, brain, and emotions are extensively studied topics. Becoming an expert in one area could take a lifetime. I do think, however, that family therapists should have a good working knowledge of genes, the brain, and the body. Here are some of my recommendations on where to gain that working knowledge.

Coyne, J. A. (2010). *Why evolution is true*. Oxford: Oxford University Press.

Summary

Why Evolution is True by Jerry Coyne is a concise and clear book that discusses the theory of evolution. Specifically, he aims to show that the evidence for evolution is so strong that it is considered scientific fact. He lays out what he sees as the six proposals that must be able to be supported by evidence if the theory of evolution is true. He then details the evidence and draws conclusions about each proposal. He also talks about human evolution and the strengths and limitations of applying the theory of evolution to understanding human behavior.

Importance for Family Systems Theory

The hypothesis of family systems theory rests on the science of evolution. The ideas of autonomy and adaptation are rooted in the research that has been conducted on Darwin's theory of evolution. In other words, if there isn't evidence for propositions of the theory of evolution, then family systems theory is built on a shaky foundation. What I like about Coyne's book is that he provides this evidence in a compelling and readable way that doesn't require you to have PhD in biology to understand. What's more you can come away with a clear understanding of what theory of evolution is and what it is not.

Porges, S. W. (2011). *The polyvagal theory: Neurophysiological foundations of emotions, attachment, communication, and self-regulation*. Norton Series on Interpersonal Neurobiology. New York: WW Norton & Company.

Summary

This book pulls together a collection of writings by Stephen Porges. It contains extensive discussions of the vagus nerve and the use of the social engagement system. In addition, it provides evidence in infants and adults of how the vagus nerve regulates social engagement and discusses how the polyvagal theory can give insight into major mental health issues.

Porges has also worked with a psychotherapist in a separate book to talk about how this theory can be used in therapy. It is called, *The Polyvagal Theory in Therapy: Engaging the Rhythm of Regulation.*

Importance for family systems theory

The Polyvagal Theory is essential reading to understand the role of the individual system in the family system. It provides therapist and researchers an introduction to the biological underpinnings of social engagement and shows how the brain and body are connected when socially responding. It also shows how the brain and body evolved to help groups of humans be autonomous and adaptable systems.

Panksepp, J., & Biven, L. (2012). *The archaeology of mind: Neuroevolutionary origins of human emotions.* Norton Series on Interpersonal Neurobiology. New York: WW Norton & Company.

Summary

The Archeology of Mind by Jaak Panksepp and Lucy Bevin expands greatly on the emotion systems summarized here. In it, Panksepp and Bevin lay out evidence that they and other researchers have accumulated to support the idea of emotion systems and the psychobehavioral reactions they create. Specifically, they go through each emotion system and argue for the evolutionary sources of these emotion system. They also spend a few chapters discussing how these emotion systems may have evolved to give humans a sense of self and raise some philosophical questions.

Importance for family systems theory

This book is key to understanding the biological underpinnings and evolutionary history of the family system. The processes that bind the family system together are fear, individuality, and belongingness. Each of the emotion systems that Panksepp proposes fuel, and are often the sources of, the processes in the family system. The evidence for these emotion systems help us understand how social groups evolved and why the family is essential for survival.

Gross, J. J. (Ed.). (2013). *Handbook of emotion regulation.* New York: Guilford Publications.

Summary

The Handbook of Emotion Regulation edited by James Gross is a sweeping discussion with chapters written by some of the leading researchers in the field of emotion regulation. The chapters cover the biological bases of emotion regulation, the cognitive processes that are important in regulating emotions, and how emotion regulation develops across the lifespan. In addition, there are chapters that explore connections between emotion regulation and attachment systems and how emotion regulation might help inform psychotherapy.

Importance for family systems theory

Emotions and emotion regulation are central to family systems theory. We often feel connect in the family system because of emotions, and emotion regulation helps us sustain relationships over time. This book provides clear explanations and a strong evidence base for emotion regulation processes and talks about how emotion regulation is key to making and keeping relationships.

Conching, A. K. S., & Thayer, Z. (2019). Biological pathways for historical trauma to affect health: A conceptual model focusing on epigenetic modifications. *Social Science & Medicine, 230,* 74–82.

Summary

Andie Kealohi Sato Conching and Zanetan Theyer's article "Biological pathways for historical trauma to affect health: A conceptual model focusing on epigenetic modification" in the journal *Social Science and Medicine* provides a clear framework for therapists to understand how epigenetic factors can be translated intergenerationally. In addition, this article contains a summary of major studies and other evidence that suggest how trauma gets passed down through the epigenome. It is one of the first and clearest conceptual models of epigenetic transmission.

Importance for family systems theory

I drew heavily on this conceptual framework in applying epigenetics to family systems theory. I appreciate the clear, multi-pathway model they developed, and the simplicity allows for those who are not familiar with epigenetics to still engage with the work. What's more, they also use this model to discuss epigenetic changes that can occur because of historical and mass trauma.

Genetic Learning Center (www.learn.genetics. utah.edu)

Summary

Genetic Learning Center (www.learn.genetics.utah.edu) is a website hosted by the University of Utah that provides clear descriptions and pictures of important concepts regarding genetics. It goes beyond the discussion of genetics and epigenetics that I covered and provides details and information about genes and epigenetics that is comprehensive but accessible.

Importance for family systems theory

Many family therapists get little-to-no training regarding genetics and how genetic and epigenetic inheritance affects individuals and family systems. This website is a great introduction. It provides pictures, videos, and text that provide a foundation for understanding genes. It's also updated regularly; as new knowledge is gained through research, this website updates to provide the most accurate information.

Attachment, Triangulation, and Family Systems

To explore more about the attachment, triangulation, and family systems, here are some great books and research articles. Many of these serve as the foundation for the information I summarized.

Johnson, S. M. (2019). *Attachment theory in practice: Emotionally focused therapy (EFT) with individuals, couples, and families.* New York: Guilford Publications.

Summary

Johnson's latest book expands upon her previous work to show how emotionally focused therapy can be expanded to individuals and families. In this book, Johnson also makes an argument of using attachment theory as the basis for affective practice. She provides a concise but conceptually informative discussion of attachment theory and talks about how it can guide practice. She also argues against the common factors approach and advocates for theory-based couple and family therapy models.

Importance for family systems theory

I made the argument that family systems theory provides a better theory to build a family therapy practice on than attachment theory. Don't draw your own conclusion until you read Sue Johnson's book. In her book she makes a compelling case for attachment theory. Though her argument and the one I present in this book rest on the assumption – empirically supported theory is needed to successfully build a model of couple and family therapy – the theories we argue for are different. Understanding her argument is key to understanding the argument I make.

Dallos, R., & Vetere, A. (2012). Systems theory, family attachments and processes of triangulation: Does the concept of triangulation offer a useful bridge? *Journal of Family Therapy, 34*(2), 117–137.

Summary

"Systems theory, family attachments and processes of triangulation: Does the concept of triangulation offer a useful bridge?" by Rudi Dallos and Arlene Vetere published in the *Journal of Family Therapy* is an excellent discussion of how the attachment system and triangulation systems are connected. It is also a great resource to look for research regarding triangulation. Dallos and Vetere provide a clear, evidence-based argument for the connection between attachment and triangulation. Through their writing they show how the attachment systems that we have are overlapping and create the triangulation system.

Importance for family systems theory

I think that the concepts of triangulation and the triangulation system are some of the most valuable contributions that family therapy has made to understanding of human behavior. I also think that often, researchers and family therapists forget the importance of this system and focus instead on the attachment system. In this article, Dallos and Vetere show the connection between the two systems and emphasize the importance of triangles to understanding families.

Olson, D. H., Waldvogel, L., & Schlieff, M. (2019). Circumplex model of marital and family systems: An update. *Journal of Family Theory & Review, 11*(2), 199–211.

Summary

Though much has been written by David Olson and others about the Circumplex Model, I would recommend starting with "Circumplex model of marital and family systems: An update" published in the *Journal of Family Theory and Review*. This article is the most updated take on Olson's work and provides a good overview of research that has used this as a framework. In addition, it provides an example of how a family can change their levels of cohesion and flexibility across the life course.

Importance for family systems theory

The Circumplex Model and the FACES-IV assessment is one of the only models of family systems that incorporates autonomy and adaptation processes. Though Olson's model doesn't hypothesize or describe how the dynamics might occur within the family system, it is an excellent way to conceptualize the family system as a whole and to describe the boundary of how the family system interacts with its environment.

Mikulincer, M., & Shaver, P. R. (2007). *Attachment in adulthood: Structure, dynamics, and change.* New York: Guilford Publications.

Summary

Attachment in adulthood: Structure, dynamics, and change edited by Mario Mikulincer and Phillip Shaver explores the attachment system and provides an excellent summary of the research regarding attachment theory. Though much has been written about attachment in childhood, this book explores the evidence for attachment in adulthood. Specifically, the editors pull in experts to write chapters about the evidence of how attachment processes affect sex, parenting, and other aspects of romantic relationships.

Importance of family systems theory

Many of the experts who wrote chapters for this edited book take a different approach on the attachment system than what I have argued. In their book, a romantic attachment system is seen as the central relationship for adulthood. I have laid out my arguments as to why I don't agree. To truly understand those arguments, I think it is necessary to understand all of the research regarding attachment in adulthood. The authors of the chapters of this book make a compelling case but also highlight the limitation of attachment in adulthood.

The Sociocultural System

Family systems are products of their environments. To maintain autonomy, the family system must adapt to the environment. Though the context of each family system is different, it is important to understand the broad sociocultural forces that shape the power structures that provide privileges to some and oppress others. My focus has been almost exclusively on the processes of power, privilege, and oppression in North America – as this is the context in which I am embedded. The books and articles that follow are the same. Even though these contexts may not be applicable to all readers, I think that these books and articles do a fantastic job of also talking about the processes that lead to the development of these contexts – something, I think, is applicable everywhere.

Kendi, I. X. (2019). *How to be an antiracist.* New York: One World, Ballantine.

Summary

How to be an Antiracist by Ibram X. Kendi is an incredible book that not only provides a history lesson on racist ideas and polices but also weaves together a narrative about the author's life and ideas about how we can challenge our own racism. This book explores, primarily, racism in the United States. However, Kendi, as an historian, often talks about the historical processes that have led to race being an identity that provides privileges and oppresses.

Importance for family systems theory

Family therapists and researchers who work in the United States cannot do their work without understanding and accounting for racism. Race is one of the main sources of power in the United States. It is likely that many therapists and researchers have, at one time or another, supported racist policies or ideas. This book helps us examine the times when we have promoted racist policies and ideas and ways in which we can better espouse and practice anti-racism.

McDowell, T., Knudson-Martin, C., & Bermudez, J. M. (2017). *Socioculturally attuned family therapy: Guidelines for equitable theory and practice*. New York: Routledge.

Summary

Teresa McDowell, Carmen Kundson-Martin, and J. Maria Bermudez's book *Socioculturally Attuned Family Therapy* is one of the best books I've come across that links family therapy models and social justice ideas. Drawing on the best available evidence and the authors' lived experiences, the authors provide a way for therapists to infuse social justice principles into their practice to empower clients for broader systemic change.

Importance for family systems theory

One of the arguments I make is that to improve family therapy models, we don't need to start over or focus solely on common factors. I argue that we need to apply evidence gained by tested theoretical hypotheses that increase our knowledge of families to these models. In this book McDowell, Knudson-Martin, and Bermudez do just that. I think that the process they engage in shows us the best way forward to improve family therapy practice.

Chambers, C. (2017). *Against marriage: An egalitarian defense of the marriage-free state*. Oxford: Oxford University Press.

Summary

Against Marriage: An Egalitarian Defense of the Marriage-Free State by Clare Chambers chronicles the oppressive institution that marriage has been and continues to be even after many countries have passed marriage equality bill. It argues for an alternative – providing the rights and protections afforded to those who are married to everyone. As a lawyer, Chambers traces laws and policies that have traditionally and currently accompanied marriage and illustrates how these policies have led to privileging some while oppressing others.

Importance for family systems theory

Many family therapists work with couples and with families where partners are married. It is likely that many of them have, at one time or another, reinforced or supported polices and ideas about marriage that could lead to the oppression of many. This book makes some of these historical and current polices explicit and shows the damaging affect they may have on couples and families.

Statistical Literacy

Many therapists don't like statistics, but if you can understand just a few basic concepts of research methods and statistics, research can become much more accessible. If you are a member of the American Association for Marriage and Family Therapy (AAMFT), I recommend checking out your subscription to *The Journal of Marital and Family Therapy*. As the flagship journal of AAMFT, it provides cutting-edge research on all things family therapy. Occasionally, this journal publishes articles on statistical advances and talks about ways in which clinicians can understand these approaches. In addition, when possible, I'd also recommend getting a subscription to the journals *Family Process* and the *Journal of Family Psychology*. By reading the research articles published in these journals and the virtual issues that are hosted online, therapists can stay up to date on the research regarding family systems theory and family therapy. Here are some of the best resources that I have come across that can help you understand the quantitative research results in these journals.

Two of the most important concepts for therapists to understand are p values and effect sizes. The article "Science Isn't Broken" written by Christine Aschwanded of fivethirtyeight.com provides an excellent discussion of some of the basic aspects of statistics and how therapists can understand what it means to have a significant finding and an impactful finding. The article can be found here: https://fivethirtyeight.com/features/science-isnt-broken/?ex_cid=endlink#part1

Fivethirtyeight.com has another article, also written by Christien Aschwanded about the importance of replicating scientific findings. For something to become scientific fact, there must be evidence from multiple studies that a phenomenon exists. The article can be found here: https://fivethirtyeight.com/features/psychology-is-starting-to-deal-with-its-replication-problem/

The Kahn Academy has lots of great videos about basic statistics. I think the two most important are about hypothesis testing and regression. If you understand these two concepts, you can understand much of the current research being produced, at least in part. Videos can be found here: www.khanacademy.org/math/statistics-probability/significance-tests-one-sample and here: www.khanacademy.org/math/statistics-probability/advanced-regression-inference-transforming

Appendix B

Engage Differently

You may not have time to sit down to read a book or to decipher a research article. But there are ways that you can still engage with high-quality research and scientific discussion. I've divided this appendix by type of engagement (e.g., podcast, website, social media platform) and not by topic. That way, depending on how you consume information, you may be able to find a way to engage with science that best fits your life.

Podcasts

This is a great way to engage with science while commuting, waiting for your next client to arrive, or when in the shower. Some of these are science podcasts and others are focused on relationship science.

1. Attached Podcast is a podcast that discusses relationship research, relationship advice, and the way relationships are depicted in the media. It focuses on debunking bad relationship advice and using research-backed ways to improve your relationships. Full disclosure: I'm one of the hosts of this podcast.
2. Bad Science is a weekly podcast where a scientist and a comedian come together and talk about how science is poorly portrayed in media. This is a funny and engaging way to think about the problems with how science is discussed in movies and TV.
3. Science Rules! With Bill Nye is a podcast that seeks to answer listeners' questions about science. It covers everything from why anxiety is normal to why cephalopods are interesting.
4. The AAMFT Podcast, hosted by Eli Karam is focused of family therapist and family systems research. It provides in-depth discussions from leading thinkers, researchers, and clinicians. It helps family therapists stay up to date with research, theory, and models.
5. Where Should We Begin with Ester Perel is, in my opinion, the best psychotherapy podcast available. In it, Ester Perel sits down with

couples and families and records a therapy session. During the session it cuts away to give insight into Perel's thinking and approach.
6. Hidden Brain with Shankar Vedantam focuses on the link between the brain and behavior. It pays particular attention to the unconscious patterns that shape relationships and choices.

Social Media – Facebook, Instagram, YouTube, and Twitter

I've listed here what, in my view, are the organizations to follow on social media. Most of the organizations cover many broad topics associated with the research covered in this book. As such, I've listed only the organization's name and ways you can link to it. That way you can follow them on your preferred social media platform. This isn't an exhaustive list, but rather a jumping-off point to help you to begin to engage differently with science.

	Facebook	Instagram	Twitter
Scientific American	facebook.com/ScientificAmerican	Scientific_american	@sciam
Nature	facebook.com/nature/		@nature
Science Magazine	facebook.com/ScienceMagazine		@ScienceMagazine
New Scientist	facebook.com/newscientist		@newscientist
Psychology Today	facebook.com/psychologytoday	psyh_today	@psychtoday
AAMFT	facebook.com/TheAAMFT/		@TheAAFMT

Bibliography

Aaron, A. (2016). Why attachment theory is all sizzle and no steak. *Psychology Today*. Retrieved from www.psychologytoday.com/us/blog/standard-deviations/201608/why-attachment-theory-is-all-sizzle-and-no-steak

Acevedo, B. P., & Aron, A. (2009). Does a long-term relationship kill romantic love? *Review of General Psychology, 13*(1), 59–65.

Afifi, T. D., Davis, S., Merrill, A. F., Coveleski, S., Denes, A., & Shahnazi, A. F. (2018). Couples' communication about financial uncertainty following the great recession and its association with stress, mental health and divorce proneness. *Journal of Family and Economic Issues, 39*(2), 205–219.

Afifi, T. D., Merrill, A. F., & Davis, S. (2016). The theory of resilience and relational load. *Personal Relationships, 23*(4), 663–683.

Afifi, T. O., Enns, M. W., Cox, B. J., Asmundson, G. J., Stein, M. B., & Sareen, J. (2008). Population attributable fractions of psychiatric disorders and suicide ideation and attempts associated with adverse childhood experiences. *American Journal of Public Health, 98*(5), 946–952.

Aggarwal, B., & Mosca, L. (2009). Heart disease risk for female cardiac caregivers. *The Female Patient, 34*(2), 42.

Alcalá-López, D., Smallwood, J., Jefferies, E., Van Overwalle, F., Vogeley, K., Mars, R. B., . . . Bzdok, D. (2018). Computing the social brain connectome across systems and states. *Cerebral Cortex, 28*(7), 2207–2232.

Aldao, A., Nolen-Hoeksema, S., & Schweizer, S. (2010). Emotion-regulation strategies across psychopathology: A meta-analytic review. *Clinical Psychology Review, 30*(2), 217–237.

Amato, P. R., & Afifi, T. D. (2006). Feeling caught between parents: Adult children's relations with parents and subjective well-being. *Journal of Marriage and Family, 68*(1), 222–235.

Amodio, D. M., & Frith, C. D. (2006). Meeting of minds: The medial frontal cortex and social cognition. In *Discovering the social mind* (pp. 183–207). New York: Psychology Press.

Anderson, H. (1997). *Conversation, language, and possibilities: A postmodern approach to therapy*. New York: Basic Books.

Anderson, J. R. (2020). Inviting autonomy back to the table: The importance of autonomy for healthy relationship functioning. *Journal of Marital and Family Therapy, 46*(1), 3–14.

Bibliography 161

Anker, M. G., Duncan, B. L., & Sparks, J. A. (2009). Using client feedback to improve couple therapy outcomes: A randomized clinical trial in a naturalistic setting. *Journal of Consulting and Clinical Psychology, 77*(4), 693.

Apicella, C. L., & Silk, J. B. (2019). The evolution of human cooperation. *Current Biology, 29*(11), R447–R450.

Bailey, Z. D., Krieger, N., Agénor, M., Graves, J., Linos, N., & Bassett, M. T. (2017). Structural racism and health inequities in the USA: Evidence and interventions. *The Lancet, 389*(10077), 1453–1463.

Barnwell, A. (2019). Family secrets and the slow violence of social stigma. *Sociology, 53*(6), 1111–1126.

Baumrind, D. (1966). Effects of authoritative parental control on child behavior. *Child Development*, 887–907.

Baumrind, D. (2013). Authoritative parenting revisited: History and current status. In R. E. Larzelere, A. S. Morris, & A. W. Harrist (Eds.), *Authoritative parenting: Synthesizing nurturance and discipline for optimal child development* (pp. 11–34). Washington, DC: American Psychological Association.

Benjamins, M. R., Hirschtick, J. L., Hunt, B. R., Hughes, M. M., & Hunter, B. (2017). Racial disparities in heart disease mortality in the 50 largest US cities. *Journal of Racial and Ethnic Health Disparities, 4*(5), 967–975.

Benware, J. (2013). *Predictors of father-child and mother-child attachment in two-parent families*. Retrieved from https://digitalcommons.usu.edu/etd/1734/

Birnbaum, G. E., Mizrahi, M., Kovler, L., Shutzman, B., Aloni-Soroker, A., & Reis, H. T. (2019). Our fragile relationships: Relationship threat and its effect on the allure of alternative mates. *Archives of Sexual Behavior, 48*(3), 703–713.

Birnbaum, G. E., & Reis, H. T. (2019). Evolved to be connected: The dynamics of attachment and sex over the course of romantic relationships. *Current Opinion in Psychology, 25*, 11–15.

Blow, A. J., & Hartnett, K. (2005). Infidelity in committed relationships I: A methodological review. *Journal of Marital and Family Therapy, 31*(2), 183–216.

Borges, J. L. (1972). *Selected poems, 1923–1967*. New York: Delacorte Press.

Bowers, M. E., & Yehuda, R. (2016). Intergenerational transmission of stress in humans. *Neuropsychopharmacology, 41*(1), 232–244.

Bradshaw, G. A., Schore, A. N., Brown, J. L., Poole, J. H., & Moss, C. J. (2005). Elephant breakdown. *Nature, 433*(7028), 807.

Buehler, C., & Welsh, D. P. (2009). A process model of adolescents' triangulation into parents' marital conflict: The role of emotional reactivity. *Journal of Family Psychology, 23*(2), 167.

Buss, D. (2015). *Evolutionary psychology: The new science of the mind*. New York: Psychology Press.

Carr, A. (2014a). The evidence base for family therapy and systemic interventions for child-focused problems. *Journal of Family Therapy, 36*(2), 107–157.

Carr, A. (2014b). The evidence base for couple therapy, family therapy and systemic interventions for adult-focused problems. *Journal of Family Therapy, 36*(2), 158–194.

Carr, A. (2016). The evolution of systems theory. In T. L. Sexton & J. Lebow (Eds.), *Handbook of family therapy: The science and practice of working with families and couples*. London: Routledge.

Carr, D., & Springer, K. W. (2010). Advances in families and health research in the 21st century. *Journal of Marriage and Family*, 72(3), 743–761.
Carter, R. T., Kirkinis, K., & Johnson, V. E. (2019). Relationships between trauma symptoms and race-based traumatic stress. *Traumatology*, 26(1).
Center for Disease Control and Prevention. (2019). *Heart disease facts*. Retrieved from www.cdc.gov/heartdisease/facts.htm
Cerniglia, L., Cimino, S., Tafà, M., Marzilli, E., Ballarotto, G., & Bracaglia, F. (2017). Family profiles in eating disorders: Family functioning and psychopathology. *Psychology Research and Behavior Management*, 10, 305.
Chambers, C. (2017). *Against marriage: An egalitarian defense of the marriage-free state*. Oxford: Oxford University Press.
Chambers, J. K. (2007). Sociolinguistics. In *The Blackwell encyclopedia of sociology*. Malden, MA: Wiley Blackwell.
Chen, E. H., Shofer, F. S., Dean, A. J., Hollander, J. E., Baxt, W. G., Robey, J. L., ... Mills, A. M. (2008). Gender disparity in analgesic treatment of emergency department patients with acute abdominal pain. *Academic Emergency Medicine*, 15(5), 414–418.
Chen, R., Hughes, A. C., & Austin, J. P. (2017). The use of theory in family therapy research: Content analysis and update. *Journal of Marital and Family Therapy*, 43(3), 514–525.
Chu, P. S., Saucier, D. A., & Hafner, E. (2010). Meta-analysis of the relationships between social support and well-being in children and adolescents. *Journal of Social and Clinical Psychology*, 29(6), 624–645.
Cohen, S. (2004). Social relationships and health. *American Psychologist*, 59(8), 676.
Conching, A. K. S., & Thayer, Z. (2019). Biological pathways for historical trauma to affect health: A conceptual model focusing on epigenetic modifications. *Social Science & Medicine*, 230, 74–82.
Conger, R. D., & Elder, G. H. (1994). Families in troubled times: The Iowa youth and families project. *Families in Troubled Times: Adapting to Change in Rural America*, 3–19.
Coontz, S. (2016). *The way we never were: American families and the nostalgia trap*. London: Hachette.
Coyne, J. A. (2010). *Why evolution is true*. Oxford: Oxford University Press.
Cyranowski, J. M., Zill, N., Bode, R., Butt, Z., Kelly, M. A., Pilkonis, P. A., ... Cella, D. (2013). Assessing social support, companionship, and distress: National institute of health (NIH) toolbox adult social relationship scales. *Health Psychology*, 32(3), 293.
Dabla-Norris, M. E., Kochhar, M. K., Suphaphiphat, M. N., Ricka, M. F., & Tsounta, E. (2015). *Causes and consequences of income inequality: A global perspective*. Washington, DC: International Monetary Fund.
Dalal, F. (2018). *CBT: The cognitive behavioural tsunami: Managerialism, politics and the corruptions of science*. London: Routledge.
Dallos, R., & Vetere, A. (2012). Systems theory, family attachments and processes of triangulation: Does the concept of triangulation offer a useful bridge? *Journal of Family Therapy*, 34(2), 117–137.

Dattilio, F. M., Piercy, F. P., & Davis, S. D. (2014). The divide between "evidenced-based" approaches and practitioners of traditional theories of family therapy. *Journal of Marital and Family Therapy*, *40*(1), 5–16.

Davis, K. L., & Montag, C. (2019). Selected principles of Pankseppian affective neuroscience. *Frontiers in Neuroscience*, *12*, 1025.

Desmond, M. (2012). Disposable ties and the urban poor. *American Journal of Sociology*, *117*(5), 1295–1335.

Diamond, G., Leckrone, J. O. D. I., Dennis, M., & Godley, S. H. (2006). The cannabis youth treatment study: The treatment models and preliminary findings. *Cannabis Dependence: Its Nature, Consequences, and Treatment*, 247–274.

DiCorcia, J. A., Snidman, N., Sravish, A. V., & Tronick, E. (2016). Evaluating the nature of the still-face effect in the double face-to-face still-face paradigm using different comparison groups. *Infancy*, *21*(3), 332–352.

DiGangi, C. (2017). This man's ambulance ride cost $2,700: Is that normal? *USA Today*. Retrieved from www.usatoday.com/story/money/personalfinance/2017/05/20/ambulance-health-care-services-costs/334338001/

Doyle, A. B., Lawford, H., & Markiewicz, D. (2009). Attachment style with mother, father, best friend, and romantic partner during adolescence. *Journal of Research on Adolescence*, *19*(4), 690–714.

Duncan, B. L., Miller, S. D., Wampold, B. E., & Hubble, M. A. (2010). *The heart and soul of change: Delivering what works in therapy*. Washington, DC: American Psychological Association.

Dziengel, L. (2012). Resilience, ambiguous loss, and older same-sex couples: The resilience constellation model. *Journal of Social Service Research*, *38*(1), 74–88.

Ehring, T., & Quack, D. (2010). Emotion regulation difficulties in trauma survivors: The role of trauma type and PTSD symptom severity. *Behavior Therapy*, *41*(4), 587–598.

Ellis, G., & Solms, M. (2018). *Beyond evolutionary psychology*. Cambridge: Cambridge University Press.

Erwin, E. (1997). *Philosophy and psychotherapy: Razing the troubles of the brain*. London: Sage Publications.

Falicov, C. J. (2012). Immigrant family processes: A multidimensional framework. In F. Walsh (Ed.), *Normal family processes: Growing diversity and complexity* (pp. 297–323). New York: Guilford Publications.

Falicov, C. J. (2014). Psychotherapy and supervision as cultural encounters: The multidimensional ecological comparative approach framework. In C. A. Falender, E. P. Shafranske, & C. J. Falicov (Eds.), *Multiculturalism and diversity in clinical supervision: A competency-based approach* (pp. 29–58). Washington, DC: American Psychological Association.

Farr, R. H., Bruun, S. T., & Patterson, C. J. (2019). Longitudinal associations between coparenting and child adjustment among lesbian, gay, and heterosexual adoptive parent families. *Developmental Psychology*, *55*(12).

Felitti, V. J., Anda, R. F., Nordenberg, D., Williamson, D. F., Spitz, A. M., Edwards, V., & Marks, J. S. (1998). Relationship of childhood abuse and household dysfunction to many of the leading causes of death in adults: The

Adverse Childhood Experiences (ACE) Study. *American Journal of Preventive Medicine*, *14*(4), 245–258.

Fife, S. T. (2020). Theory: The heart of systemic family therapy. In K. S. Wampler (Ed.), *The handbook of systemic family therapy* (pp. 296–316). Hoboken: Wiley Blackwell.

Figley, C. R., and Figley, K. R. (2009). Stemming the tide of trauma systemically: The role of family therapy. *Australian and New Zealand Journal of Family Therapy*, *30*(3), 173–183.

Fishbane, M. D. (2013). *Loving with the brain in mind: Neurobiology and couple therapy*. Norton Series on Interpersonal Neurobiology. New York: WW Norton & Company.

Ford, J. D., & Courtois, C. A. (Eds.). (2013). *Treating complex traumatic stress disorders in children and adolescents: Scientific foundations and therapeutic models*. New York: Guilford Publications.

Fosco, G. M., & Grych, J. H. (2010). Adolescent triangulation into parental conflicts: Longitudinal implications for appraisals and adolescent-parent relations. *Journal of Marriage and Family*, *72*(2), 254–266.

Fosco, G. M., Lippold, M., & Feinberg, M. E. (2014). Interparental boundary problems, parent – adolescent hostility, and adolescent – parent hostility: A family process model for adolescent aggression problems. *Couple and Family Psychology: Research and Practice*, *3*(3), 141.

Fosco, G. M., Raynor, S. M., & Grych, J. H. (2004). *Triangulation, appraisals, and adjustment: Examining the impact of interparental conflict on adolescent functioning*. Poster presented at the biennial meeting of the Society for Research on Adolescence, Baltimore, pp. 614–625.

Fraser, K., MacKenzie, D., & Versnel, J. (2017). Complex trauma in children and youth: A scoping review of sensory-based interventions. *Occupational Therapy in Mental Health*, *33*(3), 199–216.

Gallese, V., Fadiga, L., Fogassi, L., & Rizzolatti, G. (1996). Action recognition in the premotor cortex. *Brain*, *119*(2), 593–609.

Geiger, A., Bente, G., Lammers, S., Tepest, R., Roth, D., Bzdok, D., & Vogeley, K. (2019). Distinct functional roles of the mirror neuron system and the mentalizing system. *NeuroImage*, *202*, 116102.

Genetic Science Learning Center. (2018, August 7). *Learn: Genetics*. Retrieved February 20, 2020, from https://learn.genetics.utah.edu/

George, M. R., Cummings, E. M., & Davies, P. T. (2010). Positive aspects of fathering and mothering, and children's attachment in kindergarten. *Early Child Development and Care*, *180*(1–2), 107–119.

Gingerich, W. J., Kim, J. S., Stams, G. J. J. M., & Macdonald, A. J. (2012). Solution-focused brief therapy outcome research. In C. Franklin, T. S. Trepper, W. J. Gingerich, & E. E. McCollum (Eds.), *Solution-focused brief therapy: A handbook of evidence-based practice* (pp. 95–111). Oxford: Oxford University Press.

Golds, L., de Kruiff, K., & MacBeth, A. (2020). Disentangling genes, attachment, and environment: A systematic review of the developmental psychopathology literature on gene – environment interactions and attachment. *Development and Psychopathology*, *32*(1), 357–381.

Gone, J. P., Hartmann, W. E., Pomerville, A., Wendt, D. C., Klem, S. H., & Burrage, R. L. (2019). The impact of historical trauma on health outcomes for indigenous populations in the USA and Canada: A systematic review. *American Psychologist, 74*(1), 20.

Gross, J. J. (Ed.). (2013). *Handbook of emotion regulation*. New York: Guilford Publications.

Grove, D. R., Greene, G. J., & Lee, M. Y. (2020). *Family therapy for treating trauma: An integrative family and systems treatment (I-FAST) approach*. Oxford: Oxford University Press.

Grych, J. H., Raynor, S. R., & Fosco, G. M. (2004). Family processes that shape the impact of interparental conflict on adolescents. *Development and Psychopathology, 16*(3), 649–665.

Gunderson, J., & Barrett, A. E. (2017). Emotional cost of emotional support? The association between intensive mothering and psychological well-being in midlife. *Journal of Family Issues, 38*(7), 992–1009.

Harandi, T. F., Taghinasab, M. M., & Nayeri, T. D. (2017). The correlation of social support with mental health: A meta-analysis. *Electronic Physician, 9*(9), 5212.

Helimäki, M., Laitila, A., & Kumpulainen, K. (2020). "Can I tell?" Children's participation and positioning in a secretive atmosphere in family therapy. *Journal of Family Therapy*. doi:10.1111/1467-6427.12296

Hoeve, M., Dubas, J. S., Eichelsheim, V. I., Van der Laan, P. H., Smeenk, W., & Gerris, J. R. (2009). The relationship between parenting and delinquency: A meta-analysis. *Journal of Abnormal Child Psychology, 37*(6), 749–775.

Hoffman, L. (2018). *Exchanging voices: A collaborative approach to family therapy*. London: Routledge.

Hsieh, J. Y., Mercer, K. J., & Costa, S. A. (2017). Parenting a second time around: The strengths and challenges of Indigenous grandparent caregivers. *Grand Families: The Contemporary Journal of Research, Practice and Policy, 4*(1), 8.

Jablonka, E., & Lamb, M. J. (2014). *Evolution in four dimensions, revised edition: Genetic, epigenetic, behavioral, and symbolic variation in the history of life*. Cambridge: MIT Press.

Jawaid, A., Roszkowski, M., & Mansuy, I. M. (2018). Transgenerational epigenetics of traumatic stress. In *Progress in molecular biology and translational science* (Vol. 158, pp. 273–298). London: Academic Press.

Johnson, L. N., Miller, R. B., Bradford, A. B., & Anderson, S. R. (2017). The marriage and family therapy practice research network (MFT-PRN): Creating a more perfect union between practice and research. *Journal of Marital and Family Therapy, 43*(4), 561–572.

Johnson, S. M. (2019). *Attachment theory in practice: Emotionally focused therapy (EFT) with individuals, couples, and families*. New York: Guilford Publications.

Johnson, S. M., Makinen, J. A., & Millikin, J. W. (2001). Attachment injuries in couple relationships: A new perspective on impasses in couples therapy. *Journal of Marital and Family Therapy, 27*(2), 145–155.

Kawabata, Y., Alink, L. R., Tseng, W. L., Van Ijzendoorn, M. H., & Crick, N. R. (2011). Maternal and paternal parenting styles associated with relational aggression in children and adolescents: A conceptual analysis and meta-analytic review. *Developmental Review, 31*(4), 240–278.

Kendi, I. X. (2019). *How to be an antiracist*. New York: One World, Ballantine.

Kent de Grey, R. G., Uchino, B. N., Trettevik, R., Cronan, S., & Hogan, J. N. (2018). Social support and sleep: A meta-analysis. *Health Psychology, 37*(8), 787.

Kerr, M. E., & Bowen, M. (1988). *Family evaluation*. New York: WW Norton & Company.

Kouneski, E. F. (2000). *Family assessment and the circumplex model: New research developments and applications* (p. 141). Twin Cities, MN: University of Minnesota Press.

Labrecque, L. T., & Whisman, M. A. (2017). Attitudes toward and prevalence of extramarital sex and descriptions of extramarital partners in the 21st century. *Journal of Family Psychology, 31*(7), 952.

Labrecque, L. T., & Whisman, M. A. (2019). Extramarital sex and marital dissolution: Does identity of the extramarital partner matter? *Family Process, 30*.

Ludwig, R. J., & Welch, M. G. (2019). Darwin's other dilemmas and the theoretical roots of emotional connection. *Frontiers in Psychology, 10*.

Maes, M., Van den Noortgate, W., Fustolo-Gunnink, S. F., Rassart, J., Luyckx, K., & Goossens, L. (2017). Loneliness in children and adolescents with chronic physical conditions: A meta-analysis. *Journal of Pediatric Psychology, 42*(6), 622–635.

Magnavita, J. J., & Anchin, J. C. (2013). *Unifying psychotherapy: Principles, methods, and evidence from clinical science*. New York: Springer Science & Business Media.

Mahner, M., & Bunge, M. (1997). *Foundations of biophilosophy*. Berlin: Springer Science & Business Media.

Mark, K. P., & Lasslo, J. A. (2018). Maintaining sexual desire in long-term relationships: A systematic review and conceptual model. *The Journal of Sex Research, 55*(4–5), 563–581.

Mastrotheodoros, S., Canário, C., Gugliandolo, M. C., Merkas, M., & Keijsers, L. (2019). Family functioning and adolescent internalizing and externalizing problems: Disentangling between-, and within-family associations. *Journal of Youth and Adolescence*, 1–14.

McDowell, T., Knudson-Martin, C., & Bermudez, J. M. (2017). *Socioculturally attuned family therapy: Guidelines for equitable theory and practice*. London: Routledge.

McEwen, B. S. (2000). Allostasis and allostatic load: Implications for neuropsychopharmacology. *Neuropsychopharmacology, 22*(2), 108.

McGoldrick, M. (2016). *The genogram casebook: A clinical companion to genograms: Assessment and intervention*. New York: WW Norton & Company.

McNeil Smith, S., & Landor, A. M. (2018). Toward a better understanding of African American families: Development of the sociocultural family stress model. *Journal of Family Theory & Review, 10*(2), 434–450.

McNelis, M., & Segrin, C. (2019). Insecure attachment predicts history of divorce, marriage, and current relationship status. *Journal of Divorce & Remarriage, 60*(5), 404–417.

Meincke, A. S. (2018). Persons as biological processes: A bio-processual way out of the personal identity dilemma. In D. J. Nicholson & J. Dupre (Eds.), *Everything flows: Towards a processual philosophy of biology* (pp. 357–378). Oxford: Oxford University Press.

Meincke, A. S. (2019). Human persons–A process view. In Was sind und wie existieren Personen? (pp. 57–80). mentis Verlag.

Mikulincer, M., & Shaver, P. R. (2007). *Attachment in adulthood: Structure, dynamics, and change*. New York: Guilford Publications.

Molix, L. (2014). Sex differences in cardiovascular health: does sexism influence women's health? *The American Journal of the Medical Sciences, 348*(2), 153–155.

Moreno, A., & Mossio, M. (2015). *Biological autonomy: A philosophical and theoretical enquiry*. Dordrecht: Springer Science & Business Media.

Neppl, T. K., Senia, J. M., & Donnellan, M. B. (2016). Effects of economic hardship: Testing the family stress model over time. *Journal of Family Psychology, 30*(1), 12.

Nixon, R. (2011). *Slow violence and the environmentalism of the poor*. Cambridge: Harvard University Press.

Olson, D. H., Olson-Sigg, A., & Larson, P. J. (2008). *The couple checkup: Find your relationship strengths*. Nashville, TN: Thomas Nelson.

Olson, D. H., Waldvogel, L., & Schlieff, M. (2019). Circumplex model of marital and family systems: An update. *Journal of Family Theory & Review, 11*(2), 199–211.

Ottersen, O. P., Dasgupta, J., Blouin, C., Buss, P., Chongsuvivatwong, V., Frenk, J., . . . Leaning, J. (2014). The political origins of health inequity: Prospects for change. *The Lancet, 383*(9917), 630–667.

Oyama, S., Griffiths, P. E., & Gray, R. D. (2001). Introduction: What is developmental systems theory. *Cycles of Contingency: Developmental Systems and Evolution*, 1–11.

Panksepp, J., & Biven, L. (2012). *The archaeology of mind: Neuroevolutionary origins of human emotions*. Norton Series on Interpersonal Neurobiology. New York: WW Norton & Company.

Papp, L. M., Kouros, C. D., & Cummings, E. M. (2009). Demand-withdraw patterns in marital conflict in the home. *Personal Relationships, 16*(2), 285–300.

Patten, E. (2016). *Racial, gender wage gaps persist in U.S. despite some progress*. Retrieved February 24, 2020, from http://pewrsr.ch/29gNnNA

Penninkilampi, R., Casey, A. N., Singh, M. F., & Brodaty, H. (2018). The association between social engagement, loneliness, and risk of dementia: A systematic review and meta-analysis. *Journal of Alzheimer's Disease, 66*(4), 1619–1633.

Perel, E. (2013). *The secret to desire in long-term relationships*. Retrieved February 21, 2020, from www.ted.com/talks/esther_perel_the_secret_to_desire_in_a_long_term_relationship/transcript?language=en

Perel, E. (2017). *The state of affairs: Rethinking infidelity-A book for anyone who has ever loved*. London: Hachette.

Piercy, F. P., & Sprenkle, D. H. (1986). Family therapy theory building: An integrative training approach. *Journal of Psychotherapy & the Family, 1*(4), 5–14.

Pilgrim, D. (2000). The real problem for postmodernism. *Journal of Family Therapy, 22*(1), 6–23.

Pinquart, M. (2016). Associations of parenting styles and dimensions with academic achievement in children and adolescents: A meta-analysis. *Educational Psychology Review*, 28(3), 475–493.
Pinquart, M. (2017). Associations of parenting dimensions and styles with externalizing problems of children and adolescents: An updated meta-analysis. *Developmental Psychology*, 53(5), 873.
Porges, S. W. (2011). *The polyvagal theory: Neurophysiological foundations of emotions, attachment, communication, and self-regulation*. Norton Series on Interpersonal Neurobiology. New York: WW Norton & Company.
Porges, S. W. (2018). Polyvagal theory: A primer. In *Clinical applications of the polyvagal theory: The emergence of polyvagal-informed therapies* (pp. 50–72). New York: WW Norton & Company.
Priest, J. B., Roberson, P. N., & Woods, S. B. (2019). In our lives and under our skin: An investigation of specific psychobiological mediators linking family relationships and health using the biobehavioral family model. *Family Process*, 58(1), 79–99.
Pugh, A. J. (2015). *The tumbleweed society: Working and caring in an age of insecurity*. Oxford: Oxford University Press.
Ramo-Fernández, L., Schneider, A., Wilker, S., & Kolassa, I. T. (2015). Epigenetic alterations associated with war trauma and childhood maltreatment. *Behavioral Sciences & the Law*, 33(5), 701–721.
Rico-Uribe, L. A., Caballero, F. F., Martín-María, N., Cabello, M., Ayuso-Mateos, J. L., & Miret, M. (2018). Association of loneliness with all-cause mortality: A meta-analysis. *PloS One*, 13(1).
Roberson, P. N., Shorter, R. L., Woods, S., & Priest, J. (2018). How health behaviors link romantic relationship dysfunction and physical health across 20 years for middle-aged and older adults. *Social Science & Medicine*, 201, 18–26.
Rosenau, P. M. (1991). *Post-modernism and the social sciences: Insights, inroads, and intrusions*. Princeton, NJ: Princeton University Press.
Rosslenbroich, B. (2014). *On the origin of autonomy: A new look at the major transitions in evolution* (Vol. 5). New York: Springer Science & Business Media.
Ruhl, H., Dolan, E. A., & Buhrmester, D. (2015). Adolescent attachment trajectories with mothers and fathers: The importance of parent–child relationship experiences and gender. *Journal of Research on Adolescence*, 25(3), 427–442.
Ryan, R. M., & Deci, E. L. (2017). *Self-determination theory: Basic psychological needs in motivation, development, and wellness*. New York: Guilford Publications.
Saban, K. L., Mathews, H. L., DeVon, H. A., & Janusek, L. W. (2014). Epigenetics and social context: Implications for disparity in cardiovascular disease. *Aging and Disease*, 5(5), 346.
Sassler, S., & Miller, A. (2017). *Cohabitation nation: Gender, class, and the remaking of relationships*. Oakland: University of California Press.
Schäfer, J. Ö., Naumann, E., Holmes, E. A., Tuschen-Caffier, B., & Samson, A. C. (2017). Emotion regulation strategies in depressive and anxiety symptoms in youth: A meta-analytic review. *Journal of Youth and Adolescence*, 46(2), 261–276.
Spunt, R. P., & Lieberman, M. D. (2012a). Dissociating modality-specific and supramodal neural systems for action understanding. *Journal of Neuroscience*, 32(10), 3575–3583.

Schnarch, D. (2009). *Intimacy & desire: Awaken the passion in your relationship*. New York: Beaufort Books.

Schrodt, P., Witt, P. L., & Shimkowski, J. R. (2014). A meta-analytical review of the demand/withdraw pattern of interaction and its associations with individual, relational, and communicative outcomes. *Communication Monographs, 81*(1), 28–58.

Seccombe, K. (2002). "Beating the odds" versus "changing the odds": Poverty, resilience, and family policy. *Journal of Marriage and Family, 64*(2), 384–394.

Seikkula, J., Laitila, A., & Rober, P. (2012). Making sense of multi-actor dialogues in family therapy and network meetings. *Journal of Marital and Family Therapy, 38*(4), 667–687.

Sexton, T. L. (2017). Functional family therapy. In *The encyclopedia of juvenile delinquency and justice* (pp. 1–7). Cham: Springer Science & Business Media.

Sexton, T. L., Ridley, C. R., & Kleiner, A. J. (2004). Beyond common factors: Multilevel-process models of therapeutic change in marriage and family therapy. *Journal of Marital and Family Therapy, 30*(2), 131–149.

Shadish, W. R., & Baldwin, S. A. (2003). Meta-analysis of MFT interventions. *Journal of Marital and Family Therapy, 29*(4), 547–570.

Shimokawa, K., Lambert, M. J., & Smart, D. W. (2010). Enhancing treatment outcome of patients at risk of treatment failure: Meta-analytic and mega-analytic review of a psychotherapy quality assurance system. *Journal of Consulting and Clinical Psychology, 78*(3), 298.

Shotter, J. (1993). *Conversational realities: Constructing life through language* (Vol. 11). London: Sage.

Singh, S., Lundy, M., Vidal de Haymes, M., & Caridad, A. N. A. (2011). Mexican immigrant families: Relating trauma and family cohesion. *Journal of Poverty, 15*(4), 427–443.

Sippel, L. M., Pietrzak, R. H., Charney, D. S., Mayes, L. C., & Southwick, S. M. (2015). How does social support enhance resilience in the trauma-exposed individual? *Ecology and Society, 20*(4).

Sparks, J. A., & Duncan, B. L. (2010). Common factors in couple and family therapy: Must all have prizes? In *The heart and soul of change: Delivering what works in therapy* (2nd ed., pp. 357–391). Washington, DC: American Psychological Association.

Spinazzola, J., Van der Kolk, B., & Ford, J. D. (2018). When nowhere is safe: Interpersonal trauma and attachment adversity as antecedents of posttraumatic stress disorder and developmental trauma disorder. *Journal of Traumatic Stress, 31*(5), 631–642.

Spiro, M. E. (1996). Postmodernist anthropology, subjectivity, and science: A modernist critique. *Comparative Studies in Society and History, 38*(4), 759–780.

Sprenkle, D. H., Davis, S. D., & Lebow, J. L. (2013). *Common factors in couple and family therapy: The overlooked foundation for effective practice*. New York: Guilford Publications.

Spunt, R. P., & Lieberman, M. D. (2012b). An integrative model of the neural systems supporting the comprehension of observed emotional behavior. *Neuroimage, 59*(3), 3050–3059.

Steele, W., & Malchiodi, C. A. (2012). *Trauma-informed practices with children and adolescents*. New York: Taylor & Francis.

Stone, C., Trisi, D., Sherman, A., & Debot, B. (2015). A guide to statistics on historical trends in income inequality. *Center on Budget and Policy Priorities, 26.*

Stringhini, S., Polidoro, S., Sacerdote, C., Kelly, R. S., Van Veldhoven, K., Agnoli, C., . . . Mattiello, A. (2015). Life-course socioeconomic status and DNA methylation of genes regulating inflammation. *International Journal of Epidemiology, 44*(4), 1320–1330.

Thayer, Z. M., & Kuzawa, C. W. (2011). Biological memories of past environments: Epigenetic pathways to health disparities. *Epigenetics, 6*(7), 798–803.

Thomas, V., & Ozechowski, T. J. (2000). A test of the circumplex model of marital and family systems using the clinical rating scale. *Journal of Marital and Family Therapy, 26*(4), 523.

Titlestad, A., & Robinson, K. (2019). Navigating parenthood as two women; the positive aspects and strengths of female same-sex parenting. *Journal of GLBT Family Studies, 15*(2), 186–209.

Tronick, E., Als, H., Adamson, L., Wise, S., & Brazelton, T. B. (1978). The infant's response to entrapment between contradictory messages in face-to-face interaction. *Journal of the American Academy of Child Psychiatry, 17*(1), 1–13.

Uchino, B. N., Trettevik, R., Kent de Grey, R. G., Cronan, S., Hogan, J., & Baucom, B. R. (2018). Social support, social integration, and inflammatory cytokines: A meta-analysis. *Health Psychology, 37*(5), 462.

Umberson, D., & Thomeer, M. B. (2020). Family matters: Research on family ties and health, 2010 to 2020. *Journal of Marriage and Family, 82*(1), 404–419.

Vallee, R. (2003). Cybernetics and systems, from past to future. *Kybernetes, 32*(5–6).

Valtorta, N. K., Kanaan, M., Gilbody, S., Ronzi, S., & Hanratty, B. (2016). Loneliness and social isolation as risk factors for coronary heart disease and stroke: Systematic review and meta-analysis of longitudinal observational studies. *Heart, 102*(13), 1009–1016.

Van der Kolk, B. A. (1996). *The body keeps score: Approaches to the psychobiology of posttraumatic stress disorder.* New York: Guilford Publications.

Verhage, M. L., Schuengel, C., Madigan, S., Fearon, R. M., Oosterman, M., Cassibba, R., . . . Van IJzendoorn, M. H. (2016). Narrowing the transmission gap: A synthesis of three decades of research on intergenerational transmission of attachment. *Psychological Bulletin, 142*(4), 337.

Vogeley, K. (2017). Two social brains: Neural mechanisms of intersubjectivity. *Philosophical Transactions of the Royal Society B: Biological Sciences, 372*(1727). doi:10.1098/rstb.2016.0245

Walsh, F. (2016). Family resilience: A developmental systems framework. *European Journal of Developmental Psychology, 13*(3), 313–324.

Wampler, K. S., Blow, A. J., McWey, L. M., Miller, R. B., & Wampler, R. S. (2019). The profession of couple, marital, and family therapy (CMFT): Defining ourselves and moving forward. *Journal of Marital and Family Therapy, 45*(1), 5–18.

Warach, B., & Josephs, L. (2019). The aftershocks of infidelity: A review of infidelity-based attachment trauma. *Sexual and Relationship Therapy,* 1–23.

Weinberg, M. K., & Tronick, E. Z. (1996). Infant affective reactions to the resumption of maternal interaction after the still-face. *Child Development*, 67(3), 905–914.

Whisman, M. A. (2007). Marital distress and DSM-IV psychiatric disorders in a population-based national survey. *Journal of Abnormal Psychology*, 116(3), 638.

White, J. M., & Epston, D. (1990). *Narrative means to therapeutic ends*. New York: WW Norton & Company.

White, J. M., Klein, D. M., & Martin, T. F. (2015). *Family theories: An introduction*. New York: WW Norton & Company.

Widom, C. S., Czaja, S. J., Kozakowski, S. S., & Chauhan, P. (2018). Does adult attachment style mediate the relationship between childhood maltreatment and mental and physical health outcomes? *Child Abuse & Neglect*, 76, 533–545.

Wiener, N. (1949). *Cybernetics*. Cambridge: MIT Press.

Willems, Y. E., de Zeeuw, E. L., van Beijsterveldt, C. E., Boomsma, D. I., Bartels, M., & Finkenauer, C. (2020). Out of control: Examining the association between family conflict and self-control in adolescence in a genetically sensitive design. *Journal of the American Academy of Child & Adolescent Psychiatry*, 59(2), 254–262.

Witherington, D. C., & Lickliter, R. (2016). Integrating development and evolution in psychological science: Evolutionary developmental psychology, developmental systems, and explanatory pluralism. *Human Development*, 59(4), 200–234.

Wittenborn, A. K., Blow, A. J., Holtrop, K., & Parra-Cardona, J. R. (2019). Strengthening clinical research in marriage and family therapy: Challenges and multilevel solutions. *Journal of Marital and Family Therapy*, 45(1), 20–32.

Woodhouse, S. S., Scott, J. R., Hepworth, A. D., & Cassidy, J. (2020). Secure base provision: A new approach to examining links between maternal caregiving and infant attachment. *Child Development*, 91(1), e249–e265.

Woods, S. B., Bridges, K., & Carpenter, E. N. (2019). The critical need to recognize that families matter for adult health: A systematic review of the literature. *Family Process*, 8.

Woods, S. B., Priest, J. B., & Roberson, P. N. (2019). Family versus intimate partners: Estimating who matters more for health in a 20-year longitudinal study. *Journal of Family Psychology*, 34(2).

Woods, S. B., Priest, J. B., & Roush, T. (2014). The biobehavioral family model: Testing social support as an additional exogenous variable. *Family Process*, 53(4), 672–685.

Yehuda, R., Flory, J. D., Bierer, L. M., Henn-Haase, C., Lehrner, A., Desarnaud, F., . . . Meaney, M. J. (2015). Lower methylation of glucocorticoid receptor gene promoter 1F in peripheral blood of veterans with posttraumatic stress disorder. *Biological Psychiatry*, 77(4), 356–364.

Yih, J., Uusberg, A., Taxer, J. L., & Gross, J. J. (2019). Better together: A unified perspective on appraisal and emotion regulation. *Cognition and Emotion*, 33(1), 41–47.

Yllö, K., & Torres, M. G. (Eds.). (2016). *Marital rape: Consent, marriage, and social change in global context*. Oxford: Oxford University Press.

Young, I. M. (2004). The five faces of oppression. In R. Heldke & P. O'Connor (Eds.), *Oppression, privilege, and resistance: Theoretical perspectives on racism, sexism, and heterosexism.* New York: McGraw-Hill Humanities Social.

Yu, M., Linn, K. A., Shinohara, R. T., Oathes, D. J., Cook, P. A., Duprat, R., . . . Fava, M. (2019). Childhood trauma history is linked to abnormal brain connectivity in major depression. *Proceedings of the National Academy of Sciences, 116*(17), 8582–8590.

Index

AAMFT Podcast 158
abuser entrapment 128
acceptance 27
adaptations 31; in family system 76–81; senses of 75–76; *see also* autonomy, and adaptation
adverse childhood experiences (ACEs) 118
affairs 39–41, 77
"affective attack" behaviors 24
affective neuroscience 23
Afifi, T. 78, 80
Against Marriage (Chambers) 53, 155–156
aggression 34
Ainsworth, M. 32
Alfonso V of Portugal, King 52
Alice in Wonderland (Carroll) 133
allostatic load 78
Anchin, J. 108
Anderson, H. 102, 103, 105
Anderson, J. 65–66, 68, 70, 112–114
anxiety 27, 118, 127
Apicella, C. 17, 70
Archaeology of Mind, The (Panksepp and Biven) 150
Aschwanded, C. 156–157
atomic theory 4
Attached Podcast 158
Attachment in Adulthood (Mikulincer and Shaver) 32, 154
attachment system or theory 13, 31–37, 79, 81; attachment injuries in 122; as bonding theory 109; couples 34–36; family systems theory and 108–116; genetic and individual system 36–37; individuality processes 112–115; insecurities of 109–115; interactions in 32; parenting 33–34; relationship complexity 110–112; secure base problem 110–112; trauma and 121–123
Attachment Theory in Practice (Johnson) 108, 134, 152
attack–attack cycle 34–35
autonomy, and adaptation: in attachment system 37, 113; in family system 7–10, 65–66, 142; in genetic/cellular system 15, 19; in sociocultural system 59–60; in triangulation system 41–42
avoidance 27

Bad Science Podcast 158
Bailey, Z. D. 58
balance hypothesis 43, 71
Barnwell, A. 123
Barrett, A. 112
Baumrind, D. 33–34
belonging: and connection 142; and individuality processes 69–71, 77, 114; and togetherness 68
Benjamins, M. R. 58
Bermudez, M. 49, 137, 155
betrayals 122
biological autonomy 66
Biological Autonomy (Moreno and Mossio) 9, 147–148
"Biological pathways for historical trauma to affect health" (Conching and Thayer) 151
biological systems 9, 94–96, 146
biological theories 142
Birnbaum, G. 35, 40
Biven, L. 24–26, 150
bodies, brains and 120, 142

Body Keeps the Score, The (van der Kolk) 120, 121
bonding theory 109
Borges, J. L. 90
boundaries and responses 10, 34
Bowen, M. 1, 2, 6, 9, 41, 48, 68, 69, 81, 132
Bowlby, J. 32, 108
brain 21–22, 105, 120, 142
Bunge, M. 75
Buss, D. 94–95

calluses 94
Cannabis Youth Treatment Study 133
CARE system 25
Carr, A. 5, 9, 48, 67, 148
Carroll, L. 133
Carter, R. 127
cells, genes and 16, 18
Centers for Disease Control and Prevention 118
Chambers, C. 53–54, 155–156
chaos and ambivalence cycle 35
child mortality rate 57
children: in attachment systems 37; interaction between parents and 31, 36, 111; social support and well-being for 87; trauma treatment for 121
Chu, P. S. 87
"Circumplex model of marital and family systems" (Olson, Waldvogel, and Schlieff) 153
Circumplex Model, Olson's 42–45, 71, 125
Clinical Rating Scale 43
cohesion 42, 44
"common factors" of change 134–135
communication 42–43
complex trauma 118
Conching, A. K. S. 19, 118, 151
construction: development as 92; evolution as 92
context sensitivity and contingency 91
Conversation, Language, and Possibilities (Anderson) 102
Coontz, S. 77
cooperation 17
cortisol 78
couples, attachment interactions in 34–36

Coyne, J. 16, 86, 149
criticize–withdraw cycle 34
cultural imperialism 51
cybernetics and systems 6
cyclomorphosis 76

Dabla-Norris, E. 56
Dallos, R. 37–39, 79, 153
Davis, S. 78
deaths, associated with heart disease 58
delinquency 34
demandingness 33
demand–withdraw pattern 34
depression 27, 118, 120, 127
desire 35–36
Desmond, M. 56, 77
developmental systems theory (DST) 90–93
development as construction 92
de Zurara, G. 52
Diamond, G. 133
DiGangi, C. 59
disconnection 33, 34
distressed romantic partnerships 38
distributed control 92
"dodo verdict" 133–134
Doyle, A. B. 32
DSM-5 128
Duncan, B. 134

economic hardship 80
eight senses of adaptation 75–76
Ellis, G. 23, 24, 25
emotional involvement 40
emotional system 6, 9
emotions 23–26; CARE system 25; FEAR system 25, 28; generation 27; identifying 22; LUST system 24; PANIC/GRIEF system 25, 28; PLAY system 25–26; RAGE system 24–25; regulation 26–28, 67; SEEKING system 23–24; six regulation strategies 27; WPVA loops 27, 28
environment: family system and 49, 76, 79–81; organism and 8, 15, 18–19, 75, 92–93
epigenetic inheritance 19, 28
epigenetics 18–19
"Episte-Weenie" game 140
Epston, D. 102, 103, 105

evidence-based practice 2, 10
evolution: as construction 92; and genetics 15; process of 15–16
evolutionary psychology 94
Evolution in Four Dimensions (Jablonka and Lamb) 18
Evolution of Systems Theory, The (Carr) 148
Exchanging Voices: A Collaborative Approach to Family Therapy (Hoffman) 102
exploitation 50
extended inheritance theme, of DST 91–92
extramarital sex 40, 41
extratherapeutic factors 134

face-heart connection 21
family: as adaptable system 75–82; as autonomous system 65–74; resilience 93; system functioning, dimensions in 42–43; therapy models 131–139
Family Adaptability and Cohesion Evaluation Scale (FACES) 43, 44
Family Evaluation (Kerr and Bowen) 1, 69
family systems theory: attachment theory and 108–116; autonomy and adaptation 7–10; biological explanations of human behavior 94–96; case example 84–86; case for 106–107, 115; connections between systems 89–94; debating 141–143; defining 4–5; evidence-based practice 2, 10; explanation of 3–4, 83; family therapy models and 131–139; future of 96–97; general systems theory and 7; great psychotherapy debate and 133–135; hypotheses 9–10; limitations of 86–87; postmodern critique and 101–107; practice-based evidence 3; proposals of 5–6; reasons for 6; revisiting 83–98; state of 1–2; survival role in 67; theory and models 135–137; trauma in 117–130; as unique system 87–89
fear 109
FEAR system 25, 28, 125
feeling system 6, 9

Fife, S. 136, 140, 141
fight-or-flight responses 20, 25
Figley, C. R. 117
Figley, K. R. 117
Fincham, F. 40
Fishbane, M. 137
flexibility 42, 44
Fosco, G. 38–39
Foundations of Biophilosophy (Mahner and Bunge) 75
Fraser, K. 120
freeze and flee cycle 35
functional family therapy 2
functional magnetic resonance imaging (fMRI) 22

Geiger, A. 22
general systems theory 7
General Systems Theory (von Bertalanffy) 5, 146
genes: and cells 16, 18; and epigenetics 142; and family system 45–46
genetic determinism 94
Genetic Learning Center 151–152
genetic system 13, 15–19; and individual system 36–37, 149–151; and trauma 118–120
Global Commission on Global Governance for Health 57
global income inequality 55–56
Golds, L. 36
Gone, J. 126–127
"good genes" 16, 19
Gray, R. 90
great recession of 2007–2009 80
Green, G. J. 117
GRIEF/PANIC system 25, 28, 68, 72
Griffiths, P. 90
Gross, J. 26, 150
Grove, D. R. 117
Grych, J. 38–39
Gunderson, J. 112

Handbook of Emotion Regulation (Gross) 150
Handbook of Systemic Family Therapy (Fife) 136
Harandi, T. F. 87
health inequities 57–58
heart disease 58
Helimaki, M. 124

Henry (the Navigator), Prince 52
Hidden Brain with Shankar Vedantam 159
historical trauma 126
Hoffman, L. 102
Homo vinculum 109
hope 134
How to Be an Antiracist (Kendi) 52, 154–155
human behavior 1, 94–96
human systems 103
hunter-gatherers 17
hypothalamic-pituitary-adrenal (HPA) axis 78, 118
hypotheses 9–10

immobilization 20
income inequality 55–56, 57
Indigenous historical trauma 126–127
individual: mind 103; model 118; pathway 19
individuality 69; and attachment system 35; and belonging processes 69–71; and flexibility 36; processes 112–115; and togetherness 6, 9, 68, 125
individual system 13, 19–28; brain 21–22; nervous system 20–21; trauma and 120–121; *see also* emotions
infidelity triangle 39–41
intellectual system 6, 9
intensive mothering 112
intergenerational: model 119; pathway 19
Inviting Autonomy Back to the Table (Anderson) 65, 112–113

Jablonka, E. 18
Jawaid, A. 119
job and income insecurity 56
Johnson, L. 3
Johnson, S. 32, 34, 68, 72, 108, 109, 122, 134, 152
Johnson, V. 127
joint determinism, of DST 91
Journal of Marital and Family Therapy, The 156

Kahn Academy 157
Kaiser Study of Adverse Childhood 118
Karam, E. 158

Kendi, I. X. 52–53, 154–155
Kerr, M. 1, 6, 41, 69, 81, 132
Kirkinis, K. 127
knowledge 104
Knudson-Martin, C. 49, 137, 155

Labrecque, L. 40
Lamb, M. 18
Landor, A. M. 59, 105
language 103–104, 105
Lasslo, J. 35
Lee, M. Y. 117
life expectancy gap, between countries 57
living systems 7, 8
loneliness 87–88
Ludwig, R. 109
LUST system 24

MacKenzie, D. 120
Maganavita, J. 108
Mahner, M. 75
major depressive disorder 120
Makinen, J. 122
Mansuy, I. 119
marginalization 50–51
marital dissolution 40
marital rape 54
Mark, K. 35
marriage 53–55
Marriage and Family Therapy Practice Network 3
marriage-free state 54
mass trauma 126, 151
Mastrotheodoros, S. 44
May, R. 40
McDowell, T. 49, 137, 155
McGoldrick, M. 90, 93
McNeil Smith, S. 105
Meincke, A. S. 8
mental health, social support and 87
mentalizing system 22, 105
Merril, A. 78
Mikulincer, M. 32, 70, 154
Millikin, J. 122
mind 103, 105
Minuchin, S. 2, 68, 131–132
mirror neuron system 22, 105
monitoring and confrontive control 33
Moreno, A. 9, 49, 147–148
Mossio, M. 9, 49, 147–148

Narrative Means to Therapeutic Ends (White and Epston) 102
natural selection 16–19, 28, 81
nervous system 20–21, 67, 121

Olson, D. 42–45, 71, 80, 125, 153
On the Origin of Autonomy (Rosslenbroich) 7, 147
oppression, five faces of 50–52, 69; cultural imperialism 51; examples 52–55; exploitation 50; marginalization 50–51; powerlessness 51; violence 51–52
optimal parenting 34
oxytocin 35
Oyama, S. 90–93
Ozechowski, T. 44

PANIC/GRIEF system 25, 28, 68, 72
Panksepp, J. 23–26, 68, 81, 150
Papp, L. 34
parent–child triangle 38–39
parenting 33–34
Perel, E. 36, 39–40, 111, 158–159
phenotypic assortment 17
physiological and emotional load 79
Pilgrim, D. 104
PLAY system 25–26
podcasts 158–159
Polyvagal Theory, The (Porges) 149–150
Porges, S. 20–21, 70, 81, 121, 149
postmodern critique: and family systems theory 101–107; problems with 104–106
power 49
powerlessness 51
practice-based evidence 3
privileges 49–50, 55
problematic flexibility 42
problem-solving 27
process, defined 66
professionals and nonprofessionals 51
protest behavior 25
protest–push/turn away–shut down interactions 34
PTSD (post-traumatic stress disorder) 118–119, 127

race-based trauma 127
racism 52–53, 58, 127
RAGE system 24–25

Ramo-Fernádez, L. 118
reappraisal 27
Reis, H. 35
relational load 78–79
relationships 102, 104, 141; attachment 33, 46, 70, 79, 115, 142; autonomy 66; complexity 110–112; infidelity in 40; romantic 31, 35, 40, 88, 111; social 21–22, 89, 104
relative adaptedness 76
reproduction 17
responsiveness 33, 36
re-traumatization 128
Roberson, P. 88
romantic partner attachment system 34–36
romantic relationships 40, 88, 111
Rosenzweig, S. 134
Rosslenbroich, B. 7–8, 49, 75, 147
Roszkowski, M. 119
Roush, T. 88
Ruhl, H. 110
rumination 27

Satir, V. 2
Schlieff, M. 153
"Science Isn't Broken" (Aschwanded) 156
Science Rules! With Bill Nye Podcast 158
secrecy 39, 123–124
secure base, idea of 110–112
SEEKING system 23–24
self: control 46; determination 69, 113; differentiation of 6, 132; sense of 32
sensitivity and responsiveness, between parents and children 36
Sexton, T. 135
sexual: alchemy 39–40; intimacy 35
Shadish, W. R. 133
Shaver, P. 32, 70, 154
Shotter, J. 101
Silk, J. 17, 70
simple trauma 118
slave trading 52
slow violence 123
Smith, S. M. 59
social: detection system 22; engagement system 20–21, 70, 121; evaluation system 22; media 159;

play 26; support 87; systems 5, 48, 50, 67, 70, 102
Sociocultural Attuned Family Therapy (McDowell, Knudson-Martin, and Bermudez) 137, 155
Sociocultural Family Stress model 59
sociocultural system 13, 48–61; autonomy and adaptation in 59–60; defined 49; power/privilege/oppression in 49–59; trauma and 126–129
Solms, M. 23, 24, 25
solution-focused therapy 2
Sparks, J. 134
stem cells 18
Still-Face experiment 31–32, 68
stress: and threats 78–79; and trauma 18–19, 125–129
stressed romantic partnership 38
stress-response processes *see* threat-response processes
substance use 40, 127
subsystems 13
suicidal ideation 126, 127
suppression 27
survival, importance of 67
system(s): autonomous and adaptable 9–10; biological 9; cybernetics and 6; defined 66; entrapment 128; genetic 13, 15–19; living 7, 8; open 132; theory 5; *see also* attachment system or theory; family systems theory; individual system; sociocultural system; triangulation systems; *specific systems*
systemic autonomy 8
"Systems theory, family attachments and processes of triangulation" (Dallos and Vetere) 153

Taylor, P. 128
Thayer, Z. 19, 118, 151
theory and research 2, 4
therapeutic alliance 134
third-order change 137
Thomas, V. 44
threat-response processes 67–69
threats and stress 78
togetherness: belonging and 68; individuality and 6, 9, 68, 125
trait autonomy 65
trauma 100, 117–118; and attachment system 121–123; category 118; in DSM-5 128; entrapment 128; and family system 125–126; and genetic system 118–120; and individual system 120–121; prevalence in childhood 118; and sociocultural system 126–129; and stress 18–19, 125–129; and triangulation system 123–124
triangulation systems 13, 37–42, 79, 81; autonomy and adaptation in 41–42; defined 37; family system 42–46; infidelity triangle 39–41; parent–child triangle 38–39; trauma and 123–124
Tronick, E. 31, 121

Unifying Psychotherapy (Maganavita and Anchin) 108
United States, health inequity in 58
University of Oslo 57

vagus nerve 21, 89
Vallee, R. 6
van der Kolk, B. 120, 121
Verhage, M. 36
Versnel, J. 120
Vetere, A. 37–39, 79, 153
violence 51–52
Vogeley, K. 22
von Bertalanffy, L. 5, 7, 66, 146

Waldvogel, L. 153
Walsh, F. 93
Wampler, K. 2, 135, 140, 141
Way We Never Were, The (Coontz) 77
Welch, M. 109
well-being: health and 87, 89; physical and emotional 54; social support and 87
Wetchler, J. 140
Where Should We Begin with Ester Perel Podcast 158–159
Whisman, M. 40
White, M. 102, 103, 105
Why Evolution Is True (Coyne) 16, 149
Willems, Y. 45
women: extramarital sex 40; income inequality 55; providing care for family members 60; reproductive process 17
Woodhouse, S. 111
Woods, S. 88
World Economic Forum 55
World Health Organization (WHO) 57
WPVA loops 27, 28, 72

Yih, J. 27
Young, I. 50–52, 126
Yu, M. 120